SS17

Experiencing
JESUS

Experiencing JESUS

John Wijngaards, MHM

Ave Maria Press   Notre Dame, Indiana

Acknowledgments

American Bible Society. The *Good News Bible,* © American Bible Society 1976. Unless otherwise indicated, all scriptural passages are from the *Good News Bible.*

Notation for other versions:

JB   *Jerusalem Bible*
AB   *Anchor Bible*
RSV *Revised Standard Version*
GP   *Grail Psalter*

Dimension Books. For excerpts from *The Mystic of Fire and Light* by G.A. Maloney, © 1975. Used with permission of the publisher.

Dimension Books. For excerpts from *Spiritual Autobiography of Charles de Foucauld* by J.F. Six, © 1964. Used with permission of the publisher.

Sheed & Ward Ltd., London. For excerpts from *The Complete Works of St Teresa of Jesus* edited by E. Allison Peers, published in 1946. Used with permission of the publisher.

J.M. Dent & Sons Ltd. For excerpts from the Everyman's Library text, one-volume edition of *The Little Flowers of St Francis, The Mirror of Perfection* and *St Bonaventure's Life of St Francis,* published in 1973. Used with permission of the publisher.

Burns & Oates, London. For excerpts from *The Story of a Soul* translated by G. M. Day, published in 1951. Used with permission of the publisher.

Routledge & Kegan Paul Ltd., London. For excerpts from *Waiting on God* by Simone Weil, published in 1963. Used with permission of the publisher.

©1981 by Ave Maria Press, Notre Dame, Indiana 46556.

International Standard Book Number: 0-87793-234-4 (Cloth)
0-87793-235-2 (Paper)

Library of Congress Catalog Card Number: 81-52295

Printed and bound in the United States of America.

Text design: Carol A. Robak
Cover design: Elizabeth French
Cover illustration: *Head of Christ* (detail), Rembrandt van Rijn

Contents

Section I
Experiencing Jesus

One
Jesus' Promise

Knowing from hearsay is one thing; experience is quite another. This is especially true about knowing people. When we say that we know someone, we normally mean a lot more than that we have heard of the person. We usually mean that we know him or her personally, that we have met, that we have had direct dealings. We cannot say we *know* someone unless we have had personal, direct experience of that person.

Fans who keep books full of photographs and biographical data of a favorite sportsman or entertainer will treasure infinitely more a few seconds of face-to-face encounter with that person. Real experience, even in a fleeting contact, means so much more than theoretical knowledge.

Why is it that we don't apply this to our knowledge of God? Why do so many people still think that *believing* consists in "accepting as true" certain information about God? Why is it that in religious instruction, preaching and spiritual books, so much stress is laid on teaching people *about* God? Are we perhaps under the impression that we shall be better Christians the more we know *of* God? But what will the average Christian say when we ask him pointblank whether he *knows* God? I remember vividly how on one occasion, as a young missionary in India, I had to address Hindu college students. One of them asked me the question: "Have you experienced God?" I was taken aback for a moment, not only because it required a personal witness, but also because no one had ever asked me that question before. Yet it is the central question if we want to test the reality of our faith.

Contrary to what many seem to think, being a Christian means knowing God personally. Experience of God is not reserved to anchorites or mystics; it is a recognizable reality in the life of every Christian. In this chapter I will show that Jesus himself promised such an experience to every one of his followers.

Witnesses

The early church accorded a special place of honor to the apostles and others who had known Jesus personally. They were known as "eyewitnesses" (Lk 1:2) or "those who have seen the Lord" (Polycarp). These privileged witnesses played a special role in announcing the Good News (Acts 10:39-42). John the Evangelist was one of them. Frequently he stressed that he had direct access to the facts. "The one who saw this happen has spoken of it. . . . What he said is true, and he knows that he speaks the truth" (Jn 19:35). "We write to you about the Word of life. . . . We have heard it, and we have seen it with our eyes; yes, we have seen it, and our hands have touched it" (1 Jn 1:1).

When in those early years a community of Christians would come together to celebrate the eucharistic meal on a Sunday, it must have been a great thrill to have one of these eyewitnesses present. We may well imagine that the person would be invited to narrate a personal experience of Christ and that questions would be asked about the historical circumstances of Jesus' words or deeds. Meeting an eyewitness, one who had seen the Lord, was like shaking hands with a well-known television star.

The prominence of such eyewitnesses, however, also had its drawbacks. For one thing, contact with them was bound to diminish as the years went by and

Christian communities became more widely scattered. Secondly, too much attention given to the few who had known Jesus in Palestine might leave ordinary Christians with a sense of frustration. Indians have a proverb: "No plant will grow under the banyan tree." Stress on the privileged knowledge of the few eyewitnesses might make the ordinary Christian's knowledge of Jesus look inadequate.

The New Testament repeatedly refers to this problem. Being able to testify to the facts of Jesus' life has value for the gospel; but the direct experience of Christ, which every Christian can have, is much more valuable. Paul says, "Even if at one time we judged Christ according to human standards, we no longer do so" (2 Cor 5:16). In the famous episode with Thomas, Christ says, "Do you believe because you see me [in the flesh]? How happy are those who believe without seeing me [in this way]!" (Jn 20:29). In other words, there is another way of knowing Jesus much more desirable than having seen him at work in Nazareth or Jerusalem.

Confronted with this problem, the early Christians will have asked the questions that also come to us: What is this special knowledge of Jesus which everyone can have? Can we too know him personally in some way or other? How can we be sure that he is with us? In what way can we recognize his presence? Has Jesus himself said anything about this?

It is mostly in St. John's gospel that we find answers to these questions. We know John wrote his gospel much later than the other evangelists. Whereas Matthew, Mark and Luke tried to present Jesus' words and deeds in a way that would help new converts to believe in him, John paid more attention to the problems of those who had been Christians for a long time. In particular, John devoted a great part of his gospel to describing aspects of the Christian's union with Christ.

Jesus' Words at the Last Supper

For our present purpose one particular passage stands out. It contains a very clear promise on the part of Jesus that he will make his presence known to each and every Christian worthy of the name. The text is so full of meaning that it deserves a thorough examination.

verse 18   "I shall not leave you as orphans:
I am coming back to you.

verse 19   In just a little while the world will not see me anymore; but *you will see me* because I have life and you will have life.

verse 20   On that day you will recognize
that I am in the Father,
and you are in me, and I in you.

verse 21   Whoever keeps the commandments that he has
from me is the man who loves me;
and the man who loves me will be loved by my Father,
and *I shall love him*
and *reveal myself to him.*"

verse 22   "Lord," said Judas (not Judas Iscariot), "what can have happened that you are going to reveal yourself
to us and not to the world?"

verse 23   Jesus answered,
"If anyone loves me,
he will keep my word.
Then *my Father will love him,*
and *we shall come to him*
and *make our dwelling place with him*"
(Jn 14:18-23, AB, italics added).

Let us remember the context of these words. Jesus was speaking to his apostles at the Last Supper, at the close of his public ministry. He was about to die, rise and be taken up to heaven. In one way he was taking leave of his disciples. Yet in another way — and this seems exactly the point he was making — there was no need for him to take leave. He would be coming back. He would return and remain present to his disciples.

What did Jesus mean by this "return," by this lasting presence? Different suggestions have been made:

(a) Jesus referred to the *apparitions* after the resurrection. The apostles would see him alive again in spite of his crucifixion and death.

(b) Jesus meant his return at the end of time, the *parousia,* when he would show himself "sitting at the right side of the Almighty and coming on the clouds of heaven!" (Mt 26:64).

(c) Jesus promised a very real but *spiritual* presence recognizable in the consciousness of his disciples.

A careful reading of Jesus' words excludes the first two possibilities. First of all, Jesus cannot have referred just to the apparitions. He appeared after his resurrection only to a limited number of persons and that in the course of just a few weeks' time; but the promise of Jesus' return is unrestricted. Twice (both in verses 21 and 23) Jesus promises to reveal himself to *anyone* who keeps his commandments. This promise was directed not only to his apostles, but to all those who were to believe in him through their preaching and to all his future disciples without restriction (Jn 17:20).

Secondly, a reference to the *parousia* is ruled out because Jesus stated explicitly during his trial that his Second Coming will be public and will be seen by all (Mt 26:64). But here, at the Last Supper, he spoke of a return that would only be recognized by his disciples, not by people who don't believe ("The world will not see me anymore," verse 19).

A Spiritual Reality

Jesus' promise that he will return and be present to the disciples must be taken, therefore, to point to a spiritual presence that will form part of their Christian experience. This is not an exceptional interpretation of the text. B. Lindars sums up his view of Jesus' return in these words: "It is a form of manifestation which is not accessible to the world (hence not the Parousia), nor confined to a privileged few among Christians (hence not a Resurrection appearance), but is open to all who have the right disposition for union with God. *It must, then, be an interior apprehension of Jesus and the Father in the hearts of those who love Jesus.* This can hardly be a mystical experience of an esoteric kind, which would not be accessible to all."[1]

J. H. Bernard points out that Jesus' self-revelation possesses also a strictly personal aspect. It implies the illumination of the heart of the individual disciple. Jesus says, "I will manifest myself to *him*," not to the world. Bernard sums up the whole passage as containing "the assurance that he will, in truth, manifest himself to every loving and obedient disciple."[2]

Another commentator, J. Keulers, calls Jesus' return to his disciples a mystical experience. By this, Keulers does not mean that this experience is reserved to a few with extraordinary spiritual gifts, but that the experience lies on the unspeakable level of man's encounter with God.[3]

Perhaps the most penetrating and extensive Catholic commentary on St. John's gospel in recent years was written by R.E. Brown. In his exposition of the verses we have been considering, Brown comes to the same conclusion we arrived at, but allows for various stages in the transmission and understanding of Jesus' words. He writes:

> It is obvious that Jesus is speaking of a more continued presence than was possible in the brief period of post-resurrectional appearances—not only the words "I shall not leave you orphans" but the whole tone of his remarks imply permanency. Therefore, if originally these verses referred to Jesus' coming back in a series of post-resurrectional appearances, they were soon

reinterpreted in Johannine circles to refer to a more abiding and non-corporeal presence of Jesus after the resurrection. . . . This reinterpretation grew out of the profound insight that the real gift of the post-resurrectional period was a union with Jesus that was not permanently dependent on bodily presence.[4]

In short, Brown maintains (and rightly, perhaps; one should read his whole exposé) that Jesus' promise was first understood to refer to the apparitions; and that the full sense of pointing to his permanent presence was realized somewhat later. Such a growth in awareness within the early Christian community is only natural and can be documented by other examples. For our purpose it may be sufficient to note that such a gradual unfolding and deepening of meaning does not weaken the fundamental fact of Jesus' promise. On the contrary, it strengthens it. Jesus said: "I have much more to tell you, but now it would be too much for you to bear. When, however, the Spirit comes, who reveals the truth about God, he will lead you into all the truth" (Jn 16:12-13). It is important for us to realize that John, when giving us Jesus' words at the Last Supper, presents them in such a way that we could not possibly fail to interpret them as promising Jesus' real, spiritual presence to every Christian. This is what John, writing under the inspiration of the Holy Spirit, wanted us to understand. And he wanted us to know that his had been Jesus' intention, that this is what Jesus had really meant (even if, in the beginning, some people had interpreted his words as referring to the apparitions). Jesus' words: "I am coming back to you. . . . I will reveal myself to you," are addressed to each and every one of us.

Can Jesus' Presence Be Noticed?
Accepting the obvious meaning of the verses and the agreement of many commentators that Jesus is speaking of a manifestation of himself to the individual

disciple, we should probe further and ask: What does this manifestation of Jesus consist in? And, especially, can this presence of Jesus be noticed?

Some theologians in the past linked Jesus' manifestation to the invisible presence of grace in the heart of the believer. A. Wikenhauser, for example, offered the following explanation:

> The revelation spoken of in Jn 14:22 is identical to the Father's and Jesus' coming to the believer in an invisibly spiritual manner, to the Divine persons taking their abode in the believers.[5]

But such an invisible indwelling by the Father and the Son, however precious in itself, cannot be called an *experience*. It cannot be seen, or recognized, or felt. Its presence is known to us only by faith. It does not have the impact of a face-to-face encounter. It misses the thrill of meeting a person. Did Jesus mean such a spiritual but intangible presence, or something more dramatic and subject to real experience?

I Will Reveal Myself

A study of Jesus' words makes clear that he speaks about more than just an indwelling known by faith. Take Jesus' words: "My Father will love whoever loves me; I too will love him and reveal myself to him" (Jn 14:21). When scripture says that God "reveals" himself to someone, it means that God makes that person experience his presence in a special way. Moses had worked for Yahweh and prayed to him for many years; but this knowledge was quite different from the personal encounter he had when Yahweh "revealed" himself on the mountain.

The Bible gives us a vivid description of the event:

> Moses said to Yahweh, "See, you yourself say to me, 'Make the people go on,' but you do not let me know who it is you will send with me. Yet you yourself have said, 'I know you by name and you have won my

favor.' If indeed I have won your favor, please show me your ways, so that I can understand you and win your favor." . . . Yahweh replied, "I myself will go with you, and I will give you rest." . . .

Moses said, "Show me your glory, I beg you." And he said, "I will let all my splendor pass in front of you, and I will pronounce before you the name Yahweh. I have compassion on whom I will, and I show pity to whom I please. You cannot see my face," he said, "for man cannot see me and live. . . . Here is a place beside me. You must stand on the rock, and when my glory passes by, I will put you in a cleft of the rock and shield you with my hand while I pass by. Then I will take my hand away and you shall see the back of me; but my face is not to be seen" (Ex 33:18-33,JB).

Here the Old Testament narrates a momentous experience in the life of Moses. To strengthen him for his task, God gave him something much more precious than the stone tablets of the Law inscribed by God's own finger or the external manifestations of his power in thunder and lightning on Sinai. God granted him some kind of direct encounter, an immediate communication with God's own personality, a partial but real vision of God himself. Jesus' promise in the New Testament must be understood as being of the same nature. Jesus too promises much more than external aid; he speaks of revealing himself to the disciple. "Whoever accepts my commandments and obeys them is the one who loves me. . . . I too will love him and reveal myself to him" (Jn 14:21).

This interpretation of "I will reveal myself" is consistent with other uses of this expression in the fourth gospel. In John 7:1-8 we read of a conflict between Jesus and a group of his relatives. These latter found Jesus' behavior inconsistent. If he was the Messiah, as he claimed to be, why did he not appear more visibly on the public scene? Why did he not take a more active role in religious politics and strive to create an impression in leading circles at Jerusalem?

They told Jesus:

> "Why don't you leave this place and go to Judaea so that you can show the miracles you are doing to the people there who want to follow you? If a man wants to be known he does not do things in secret. Considering what you are doing, you should *reveal yourself* to the world" (Jn 7:2-4, author's trans.).

Jesus had refused to take their advice and had stayed on in Galilee. At the Last Supper the apostles were apparently reminded of this incident when Jesus said that he would reveal himself to any person who would keep his words. We read that Judas, the Cananean, asked, "Lord, how can it be that you will reveal yourself to us and not to the world?" (Jn 14:22). Jesus' reply is tantamount to: I will not exclude anyone if only that person is ready to accept my words and so express his love for me (Jn 14:23). What we should note here is that both the apostles and Jesus himself see a clear parallel between becoming known to a wider public and the self-revelation which Jesus promises to the individual disciple. In other words, the kind of revelation that Jesus is speaking of when he says he will reveal himself is a manifestation that forces itself on the consciousness of the disciple concerned. There can be no question of Jesus secretly taking up his dwelling within the disciple's heart without the latter being able to detect it.

We Shall Make Our Dwelling Place With Him

The tangible nature of Jesus' presence in the believer can also be deduced from the way Jesus describes it as an *indwelling:*

> "If anyone loves me,
> he will keep my word.
> Then my Father will love him,
> and we shall come to him
> and make our dwelling place with him" (Jn 14:23,AB).

The Father and the Son will reside in the disciple. They will make him, as it were, their home, their palace, their temple. Could there be a question here of an indwelling that is true on the supernatural plane, but invisible to the recipient? Biblical evidence rules out such an interpretation.

God making his dwelling among human beings is a frequent theme in scripture. The theme is elaborated in a song on the Old Testament Law (Sir 24); it is applied to the Incarnation (Jn 1:13), and to the vision of heaven (Rv 21:3). But the main scriptural reality of God's dwelling with his people was Yahweh's presence in the Temple. It is described in the following terms:

> Then the cloud covered the Tent and the dazzling light of the LORD'S presence filled it. . . . They could see the cloud of the LORD'S presence over the Tent during the day and a fire burning above it during the night (Ex 40:34,38).

> [At the dedication] the Temple was suddenly filled with a cloud shining with the dazzling light of the LORD'S presence. . . . Then Solomon prayed:
> > ". . . you have chosen to live in clouds and darkness.
> > Now I have built a majestic Temple for you, a place for you to live in forever." . . .
> "But can you, O God, really live on earth? Not even all of heaven is large enough to hold you, so how can this Temple that I have built be large enough?" (1 Kgs 8:10-13,27).

What should strike us is that, for the pious Jew, God's indwelling was a visible reality: His presence radiated from the Temple. "How lovely is your dwelling place, Lord, God of hosts. . . . One day within your courts is better than a thousand elsewhere" (Ps 84:1,10,GP). Although God himself was invisible, his presence could be "seen" as a radiation of glory.

God, though invisible, was thought to be enthroned upon the cherubim that stood on top of the Ark of the Covenant (1 Kgs 6:23-28; 2 Kgs 19:15).

Wherever the Ark of the Covenant moved, there God made his presence felt. It was the Ark of Yahweh that made all Israel shout at Aphek "so that the earth resounded" (1 Sm 4:5,JB); that threw down the statue of Dagon (1 Sm 5:1-4); that struck the Philistines with tumors (1 Sm 5:6-12); that killed Uzzah for touching the lid with his hand (2 Sm 6:7); and that brought prosperity to the family of Obed Edom by its mere presence (2 Sm 6:12). God's dwelling with man was a powerful dwelling with tangible results: "The Lord is King; the peoples tremble. He is throned on the cherubim; the earth quakes. The Lord is great in Sion" (Ps 99:1,GP).

So when Jesus says, "We shall come to him and make our dwelling place with him," we have to understand it in the light of this Old Testament power and radiation of glory. We could not possibly imagine these divine guests entering our home without our noticing the difference. Their taking told of a person, their living in a person, cannot mean anything else but that they make their loving presence felt in a very profound and lasting way.

In post-scholastic theology there was a lot of discussion on the exact nature of the indwelling. With their characteristic "ontological" interest, the post-scholastics saw in it a new form of *being*. The indwelling of the Blessed Trinity was seen by them as a kind of new, special, physical superpresence, added over and above God's presence as Creator. This superpresence, however, was real on its own account; it made not the slightest difference whether it was noticed by the recipient or not. The indwelling was thought to be just as real in a baptized, newborn child as in a baptized adult.

Many centuries before, St. Thomas Aquinas had offered another interpretation that seems much closer to the biblical sources. For Thomas, the indwelling of God in the believer consists rather in a raised consciousness of mutual knowledge and love. To quote St. Thomas:

God is present in another and more specific way [different from his presence as Creator] in a rational creature who knows and loves him at a particular moment or who does so habitually. And because a rational creature can only know and love by grace, God is said in this particular manner to be present in the saints by grace.[6]

Since a rational creature through his own activity reaches God himself by knowing him and loving him, God is said according to this special way of presence not only to be in the rational creature, but even to dwell in him, as in his Temple.[7]

Mutual knowledge and love unite Jesus and his disciple. This seems to do justice to Jesus' own words:

"If anyone loves me,
he will keep my word.
Then my Father will love him,
and we shall come to him
and make our dwelling place with him" (Jn 14:23,AB).

The Father and Jesus will make their presence felt in the disciple in such a way that the disciple will feel he or she knows them better and loves them more intensely. The two verses, "I too will love him and reveal myself to him" (verse 21) and "my Father will love him, and we shall come to him and make our dwelling place with him" (verse 23) are therefore completely parallel in meaning.

Other expressions used by Jesus confirm that he is promising a tangible experience. How could Jesus say he would not leave us as orphans (Jn 14:18,JB) if his presence with us were only to be believed, not experienced? How could Jesus say, "You will see me" (Jn 14:19), unless he referred to some real perception, some recognition of his own personality? This is further confirmed because Jesus contrasts the believer's experience with the world's inability to see him. If the believer depended exclusively on intellectual knowledge derived from faith, what real advantage would he or she have over the unbeliever as far as "seeing" the Lord is concerned?

All these considerations inexorably point to the same conclusion: Jesus promised his future disciples a direct experience of himself. His words at the Last Supper may be paraphased in this way: "Although my body will ascend to heaven, I will remain present to you. You will know me, you will recognize me. In a way unintelligible to those who lack faith, you will have a direct perception of me by which you will know that we share the same life. If you remain close to me and prove your love by living my gospel, I too will show my love in a tangible manner and will make myself known to you. My Father, the Holy Spirit and I will be with you all the time, living in you, making you feel the embrace of our love."

The One Condition

In his reply to Judas, Jesus stated that he would be prepared to reveal himself to his disciples (Jn 14:23). But he repeated the same condition he had put before, namely, that such a disciple would have to keep his commandments (cf. Jn 14:21). It is as if Jesus told us in plain English: "You will experience my presence only if you. . . ." Understanding what condition he is demanding is obviously of the greatest importance. We could raise a number of questions about it: Does Jesus always require the same condition? What exactly does this condition consist in? What does it require from us? Is it possible for us today to fulfill this condition?

Studying the New Testament writings, we find five passages, in which the promise of the experience of God is linked to a condition. All five texts are Johannine and so reflect St. John's theology. It is rewarding to compare them (all texts are from AB, italics added).

Jn 14:15-17	"If you love me and *keep my commandments*,then at my request the Father will give you another Paraclete to be with you forever. He is the Spirit of Truth whom the world cannot accept since it neither sees nor recognizes him; but you do recognize him since he remains with you and is within you."
Jn 14:21	"Whoever *keeps the commandments* that he has from me is the man who loves me; and the man who loves me will be loved by my Father, and I shall love him and reveal myself to him."
Jn 14:23-24	"If anyone loves me *he will keep my word.* Then my Father will love him, and we shall come to him and make our dwelling place with him. Whoever does not love me *does not keep my words.*"
1 Jn 3:24	*Whoever keeps his [Jesus'] commandments* lives in God and God lives in him. We know that he lives in us by the Spirit that he has given us.
1 Jn 2:3-4	We can be sure that we know God only by *keeping his commandments.* Anyone who says, "I know him," and *does not keep his commandments,* is a liar, refusing to admit the truth.

In all these texts we find the promise that we shall have a direct and intimate knowledge of the Blessed Trinity: Father, Son and Holy Spirit. There may be slight differences in the way we experience the action of these Divine Persons (about which I will speak in later chapters), but fundamentally it remains one experience of the Divine. In fact, we could not possibly be aware of Jesus without remembering his relationship to the Father and participating in the Spirit whom he gives us. In all five texts the same condition is repeated: We should keep Jesus' commandments (alternative formulation: keep his word). This repetition, especially in the writings of an author like St. John who prefers synonyms and parallel formulations whenever possible, shows that we have to take it as a rather specific and exclusive condition. Jesus did not say: "If you are baptized. . . ."; "If you believe . . . ."; "If you follow me . . . ."; "If you pray regularly . . . ." His words were precise: "If you keep my commandments. . . ." The exclusive nature of this condition may also be seen in the affirmation of the opposite: Those who do not keep Jesus' commandments, do not participate in the revelation of love (Jn 14:24; 1 Jn 2:4). We can experience the Blessed Trinity in this special way *only* if we keep Jesus' words.

Fidelity to the Law?

What did Jesus mean by "keep my commandments"? Perhaps the condition strikes us as an anticlimax. Perhaps it deflates our enthusiasm by its apparent simplicity. This is because "keeping the commandments" evokes in us the picture of the law-abiding religious zealot who worries all day about loyal obedience to external rules. But, surely, this kind of legal obedience, this fidelity to the law, could never have been held out by Jesus as the supreme virtue, much less as the condition for a living and dynamic experience of God!

Jesus knew the legalism of the scribes and the Pharisees only too well. Jesus and the disciples were frequently accused by them of not observing the commandments conscientiously; of profaning the sabbath by picking corn from a field, by curing the sick or allowing a man to carry his mattress; of not following the ritual prescriptions for the washing of hands; of not fasting on traditional days; and the like. Jesus utterly rejected such an attitude toward the commandments. He called the Pharisees blind guides and hypocrites. He ridiculed their practice as "straining out gnats and swallowing camels!" (Mt 23:24,JB). He stated bluntly that prostitutes had a better chance of entering the kingdom of heaven than they (Mt 21:31) and declared the humble sinner a greater friend of God than the law-abiding, but proud, Pharisee (Lk 18:14). The last thing Jesus would want to do is to present the scrupulous observance of rules and prescriptions as the ideal he had in mind. Blind obedience, loyalty to the letter of the law, rigorous observance, the discipline of soldiers and moralists, may occasionally have raised their head even in forms of Christian spirituality: They were always far from the mind of Jesus.

Jesus' Own Commandment

To understand what Jesus means by "keep my commandments" we should stress the *my*. Jesus admitted the validity of the Ten Commandments and the basic requirements of the Old Testament Law. He did not reject them, but repeatedly stated that they were presupposed in his kingdom. "Do not think that I have come to do away with the Law of Moses and the teachings of the prophets" (Mt 5:17). "Keep the commandments if you want to enter life" (Mt 19:17). "You neglect to obey the really important teachings of the Law, such as justice and mercy and honesty. These you should practice, without neglecting the others" (Mt 23:23). On each of these occasions Jesus mentions fidelity to the laws in passing, as a first step. Never does he make it the central burden of his message.

When Jesus speaks of "my commandments," he means requirements that go beyond natural virtue or Old Testament Law. This is his main theme in the Sermon on the Mount. "Eye for eye and tooth for tooth," reward or punishment according to strict merits, is a generally accepted principle of morality. But Jesus requires more. He wants us to be magnanimous even if we are treated unjustly: by offering the other cheek, by giving our inner garment too, by carrying a burden an extra mile. He wants us not just to avoid murder, but even angry thoughts. He wants us to love not only our friends, but even those who make life difficult for us. He opposes what was said to "the men of old" (the Ten Commandments) to "I say this to you" (his own commandment). It is as if he says (Mt 5:21-48; Lk 6:27-38): "I want you to give more than people can demand from you in terms of strict justice. I want you to be kind even in your thoughts. You should be generous. You must overcome evil by good. Do not take revenge. Wish well even to your opponents. Be helpful to everyone. Love all people whatever their disposition toward you may be."

Jesus' commandments amount not to a list of rules, but to a new attitude, actually to one commandment. And this new attitude can be summed up in terms of love, the kind of love that Jesus himself exemplified. This is stated explicitly in the writings of St. John.

"I am giving you a new commandment:
Love one another.
As I have loved you,
so you too must love one another" (Jn 13:34,AB).

"This is my commandment:
Love one another
as I have loved you. . . .
This I command you:
Love one another" (Jn 15:12,17,AB).

This is the commandment that he has given us,
that anyone who loves God must also love his brother
(1 Jn 4:21, AB).

Jesus' commandment demands a love of our neighbor that springs from God; that is merciful, generous and life-giving as God's love is. It demands that we be ready to lay down our lives for it (Jn 15:13). It requires that we live the kind of life Jesus lived.

We can be sure
that we are in God
only when the one who claims to be living in him
is living the same kind of life as Christ lived (1 Jn 2:5-6,JB).

We started this chapter by asking the question whether we can know God directly and personally. The answer is yes! Jesus himself assured us that we can. His promise might be freely rendered in this way: "If any one of you really loves me and proves this love by living the kind of life I lived, I in turn will give tangible proof of my love. I will make you experience my presence."

Two
Jesus' Word and Jesus' Spirit

Jesus promised that he would manifest himself to every person faithful to his word. "I will love him and reveal myself to him" (Jn 14:21). "The Father and I will make our dwelling place with him" (Jn 14:23,AB). Jesus promised to make himself known in a tangible manner. The time has come to examine this promise more closely.

If Jesus is God—as we Christians believe—what is the difference, if any, between experiencing Jesus and experiencing God in general? Is there anything distinctive in Christian experience above and beyond the general experience of God? Have Christians their own way of experiencing God?

Another range of questions concerns the actuality of this experience. In what way does Jesus reveal himself to us? What does the experience of Jesus look like in everyday terms? How can we recognize it? Is it compatible with our 20th-century existence? Can it be described in plain, everyday language?

Since we are moving into that region of existence where many things are beyond words, we cannot hope to adequately express them just by talking about them. Yet I believe that, even here, plain language is highly desirable at all times. Spiritual realities are often emasculated by the use of antiquated or woolly terms. If religious claims are confused, indefinite or simply unintelligible, how are people expected to act on them?

To make the words of Jesus meaningful to us we have to rephrase them in terms of our own experience. St. John's gospel portrays Jesus as the voice of God, the living water and the one who leaves us his spirit. As we shall see, these three roles of Jesus help us to understand how we can experience Jesus in our lives. But before we get to the bottom of things, a real job of translation needs to be done.

The Voice of God

As we turn to St. John's gospel for enlightenment, we may begin with a fundamental question: In what way did Christ reveal God? If we are to understand Christ, we should grasp his mode of divine revelation. How did people who met Christ meet God?

We are tempted, perhaps, to rush forward with the answer. We might contend, for instance, that everything Christ said or did points to the Father. His mode of revelation was through his humanity. However attractive such a contention may look, it proves to be a fallacy. Christ's neighbors in Nazareth did not recognize God in him. There must have been something much more specific than Christ's human appearance and ordinary external actions. Being like other people in all these things, he could not through them reveal God in a special way.

Well, you might think, what about the miracles? Christ showed the power of his Father through the "works" he performed. While there is some truth here (Jn 5:36), this approach also misses the point. Christ did not appear first and foremost as a miracle worker. Christ's miraculous powers were not exercised to elicit faith; rather, they presupposed faith. Christ rebuked the official of Capernaum with the words: "None of you will ever believe unless you see miracles and wonders" (Jn 4:48). It was not through his miracles that Christ revealed his Father.

When we page through the chapters of St. John's gospel we find it stated again and again that Christ revealed his Father by *speaking*. "We speak of what we know and report what we have seen" (Jn 3:11). "The one who sent me, however, is truthful, and I tell the world only what I have heard from him" (Jn 8:26). "I say only what the Father has instructed me to say" (Jn 8:28). "What I say, then, is what the Father has told me to say" (Jn 12:50). The fullest definition is found in these words:

> The one whom God has sent
>   speaks God's words,
> because God gives him
>   the fullness of his Spirit (Jn 3:34).

What does this mean? To paraphrase it: Jesus was an ordinary carpenter in appearance; he looked like his fellow Jews in every respect. But in two ways he was marked off as distinct from others: He spoke a powerful message of love; he was seen to be full of the Holy Spirit. By the combination of these two manifestations Jesus revealed God. A spiritual person could not fail to recognize the divine presence. "He who comes from God listens to God's words" (Jn 8:47). People may at first have been drawn to listen to Christ out of curiosity; at that stage of their acquaintance he was no more for them than a man reputed to be a prophet, a carpenter turned "rabbi." Then, listening to his words and sensing God's spirit vibrating in his personality, it might suddenly dawn on them: Here, God is speaking to me! Faith meant accepting Jesus' word as true (Jn 5:24), recognizing the Father in Jesus' Spirit and in his words (Jn 14:10-11).

Jesus revealed the Father by being his Father's voice. Jesus was God's message of love (1 Jn 4:7-12). When John tries to characterize Jesus in his prologue, he doesn't call him "God's face," but "the Word." It was as the Word that Christ came into the world, that he was made flesh and lived among us (Jn 1:9,14). Jesus' whole life and mission could, in fact, be summed up in terms of communication. In everything he said and did, what mattered was the expression of a

Jesus' Word and Jesus' Spirit

divine response to man's longings, a reassurance and promise. Christ was a Word full of power, a Word that judges (Jn 12:48), a Word that cleanses (Jn 15:3), a Word that makes man free (Jn 8:31-32); but most of all, and above all, he was a Word that revealed. "No one has ever seen God. The only Son, who is the same as God and is at the Father's side, he has made him known" (Jn 1:18).

The implications of this gospel teaching are far-reaching. For the evangelist, Jesus was, first and foremost, communication. Christians are saved by accepting him as the message and by applying the touch of his saving word to their lives. Compared to this aspect of Christ, all other factual realities are insignificant. Disciples do not get closer to Jesus by having seen his physical likeness, by having touched his actual body, or by having visited the places where he stayed. Following Christ does not consist in repeating Christ's external deeds: his work as a carpenter or his miraculous healing. No, all such things are only of secondary importance. "What gives life is God's Spirit; man's power is of no use at all. The words I have spoken to you bring God's life-giving Spirit" (Jn 6:63). What counts is that Jesus is the voice of the Father, that he speaks to us through his word and his Spirit.

Jesus the Rabbi

We should never forget that throughout his public life Jesus acted as a rabbi. The function of a rabbi was well-defined in his day. The rabbi was the teacher of Jewish religion. Each rabbi gathered around him a group of disciples who received his teaching and learned it by heart. To facilitate this process, rabbis had worked out their own educational system. After explaining a point of doctrine at length, they would summarize it in short, pithy statements that could easily be memorized by the disciples. To call someone a "rabbi" in Jesus' days was as well-defined and precise as when we today say of a person that he or she is "a dentist," "a shop steward," or a "high school principal."

Jesus was acknowledged to be a rabbi even by his adversaries. Just like other rabbis, he too attracted disciples. At times his disciples are explicitly compared to those of the Pharisees. Why do your disciples act like this whereas the disciples of the Pharisees act thus? (cf. Mk 2:18). Jesus too made his disciples learn parables and short statements. When instructing his disciples he gave summaries of his doctrine just as other rabbis did.[1] Jesus consciously acted like a rabbi because that is what came closest to what he wanted to be. "You call me Teacher and Lord, and it is right that you do so, because that is what I am" (Jn 13:13).

Jesus, of course, did not fit the pattern of his colleagues in every respect. As a rabbi he deviated significantly. But when he was different, it was not by renouncing any of his status as rabbi. On the contrary, he acted as someone more "rabbi" than others, as a "super rabbi." Other teachers relied heavily on tradition; Jesus taught with authority (Mk 1:22). Jesus claimed everlasting validity for his teaching: "Heaven and earth will pass away, but my words will never pass away" (Mt 24:35). Everything must recede in the face of his words: care of one's relatives (Mk 3:31-35), praise of his mother (Lk 11:27-28), duties of hospitality (Lk 10:38-41). Jesus' word is the gateway into the kingdom (Mt 7:13). Whoever builds on Jesus' word will be saved at the last judgment (Mt 7:24-27); whoever rejects his word will be condemned (Mt 21:28-31). "Whoever rejects me and does not accept my message has one who will judge him. The words I have spoken will be his judge on the last day!" (Jn 12:48). Jesus was indeed a rabbi, but one who taught with extraordinary authority.

Jesus as the rabbi confirms what we have seen above about his principal role as the voice of God, the Word, the revelation of the Father's love. It is through his teaching that he revealed the Father. To his contemporaries Jesus manifested God's nearness by speaking as a rabbi. Will it also be the way in which he is manifesting his divinity to us? Yes, indeed. This is the implication of Jesus' parting words in Matthew's gospel: "Go, then, to all peoples everywhere and make them my disciples" (Mt 28:19). Jesus' promise, "And I will be with you always, to the end of the age," is closely related to his remaining with them through his commands which future disciples will have to learn and obey. "Teach them to obey everything I have commanded you." Jesus will be present to us as the Teacher.

Living Water

How this should happen in practice is explained through an illuminating passage in John. Jesus joined the festive crowd in the Temple on the seventh day of the Feast of Tabernacles. This was the day when according to custom a special procession marched from the fountain of Gihon to the altar of holocausts in front of the tabernacle. When the priest filled a golden pitcher with water, choirs sang: "With joy you will draw water from the wells of salvation" (Is 12:3,RSV). The pitcher was then carried triumphantly to the temple gate; the procession encircled the altar and poured out water into a silver funnel leading into the ground. This drawing of the life-giving water was probably an ancient rite derived from the fertility cult and prayers for rain that formed a part of Tabernacles from the days of old (Ps 84:6). In Jesus' day it had also acquired messianic significance; it referred to the stream of salvation that would flow from the Temple (Ez 47:1-12; Zec 13:1, 14:8).

At the end of this ceremony Jesus made a special announcement:

> On the last and greatest day of the festival, Jesus stood up and cried out,
>
> "If anyone thirsts, let him come to me and drink. He who believes in me (as the Scripture says), 'from within him shall flow rivers of living water.'"
>
> Here he was referring to the Spirit which those who came to believe in him were to receive. For there was as yet no Spirit, since Jesus had not been glorified (Jn 7:37-39).[2]

Jesus was speaking here as a teacher. In Jewish tradition, teaching was often compared to life-giving water. The Old Testament saying, "A person's words can be a source of wisdom, deep as the ocean, fresh as a flowing stream" (Prv 18:4) was understood mainly as describing a teacher. An ideal disciple retains the master's doctrine "as a plastered cistern which loses not a drop" (Mishna Abot 2:8). According to Rabbi Aqiba, the disciple should do more: "The disciple who is beginning is like a well who can give only the water it has received; the more advanced disciple a spring that gives living water."[3] When Jesus invited people to come and drink, he called on them to become his disciples. Only he, the voice of the Father, could give them the life-giving water they were praying for. As the perfect teacher, Jesus could fill his disciples with that divine knowledge that would become in them a continuous source of life and inspiration. Just as divine wisdom, a large river brimming over with water, makes rivulets and channels of her disciples (Sir 24:23-24), so Jesus turns his followers into fountains of living water.

To get the full import of this for our present-day life, the evangelist's commentary is helpful. "Here he [Jesus] was referring to the Spirit which those who came to believe in him were to receive. For there was as yet no Spirit, since Jesus had not been glorified" (Jn

7:39,AB). John is saying: Don't restrict Jesus' words to the original occasion. Don't think they were addressed only to those crowds present in the Temple on the Feast of Tabernacles. Don't believe for a minute that Jesus was just expressing a passing invitation, limited to his immediate hearers. No, here Jesus was indicating what he would do for all his disciples, especially those who were to accept his words in the future after his death and resurrection (his glorification). Jesus referred here to the Spirit he would give to all his followers so that, by a combination of his word and his Spirit, his teaching would remain in them as a source of lasting inspiration. If you follow Christ by accepting his word, you shall know you belong to him. For from within you, shall flow rivers of living water.

John was writing for Christians in Asia Minor who had been converted to Jesus long after his death and resurrection. Like us today, they had never seen Jesus. They had not heard his voice. They had little opportunity of visiting the places where he lived and died. Yet Jesus was not for them a wise teacher who had lived long before and whose doctrine had been passed down. They knew him as living and present. They were aware of his promise to reveal himself (Jn 14:21), and to be with us always, to the end of the age (Mt 28:20).

For the early Christians, Jesus' words were not just the teaching left by a dead man. Accepting Jesus' words meant acknowledging their power. Jesus was a teacher who spoke with authority; his instruction retains its force in every generation. The whole sacramental system is based on this belief. In the Eucharist it is Jesus who says, "This is my body—this is my blood" (Mt 26:27-28). In the sacrament of reconciliation it is Jesus' word that cleanses us: "Your sins are forgiven" (Mt 9:2). It is in Jesus' name that Father, Son and Holy Spirit are called down upon a person in baptism (Mt 28:19; Acts 19:5). Through the teaching authority in the church it is Jesus who speaks (Lk 10:16), Jesus who declares things lawful or unlawful (Mt 18:18). Where a community of Christians gathers and prays in his name, Jesus himself prays with them (Mt 18:19). Accepting Jesus' words means accepting also their sacramental reality today.

But there is also a subjective element of "feeling Christ's presence" well recognized by the early Christians. They knew Christ was there not just because it was a doctrine they had learned. They knew it because of the Spirit they had received. "And because of the Spirit that God has given us we know that God lives in union with us" (1 Jn 3:24). By this they meant something that is hard to define but very real to those who have experienced it. Jesus' words had not just remained a dead letter. It had sparked off a flame in their hearts. All of a sudden they *knew* Christ was in touch with them. While the words of Christ transformed them into happy persons, loving God in response to his love and trying to love their neighbors as well as they could, they became aware of a new reality in their lives. They felt enlightened by a light which they knew was not their own. They felt attracted to doing things far beyond their natural wishes and powers. They knew themselves guided by an invisible hand. This is what Paul refers to when he speaks of being "captured" by Jesus Christ, of what it means to know Christ and the power of his resurrection (Phil 3:10-12). It was this subjective element of being aware of Jesus' Spirit at work in themselves, of sensing his power and being guided by it, that put the believer in direct touch with Jesus.

Signs of Recognition

In our dealings with other persons we have come to rely very much on visual contact. We are inclined to think we know someone if we have seen that person close up. We recognize people mainly by face and stature. Since we depend so much on visual images, seeing a person face to face or at least knowing what the person looks like seem natural elements in acquaintanceship. Because of this, we may consciously or unconsciously believe that Jesus would reveal himself most clearly to us if we could see him with our bodily eyes.

Some saints have been granted this privilege. St. Ignatius of Loyola sometimes saw Jesus in a vision as a white figure. During the first retreat after his conversion, at Manresa in 1522, he recorded the following impression:

> For a long time I often saw in prayer, with the eyes of the Spirit, Christ's humanity. I saw a figure which made the impression on me of being a body. It was neither very large nor very small. I could not distinguish separate members of the body. I often received this vision in Manresa.[4]

Later in Rome, on February 27, 1544, he had a similar vision:

> During Mass while saying the prayer "Domine Jesu Christe, Fili Dei vivi, etc.," it seemed to me in Spirit that I first saw Jesus as a white figure, that is, his humanity—while a moment later I saw him in my soul in a different manner, namely, not as before in his humanity alone but now in his totality, as God. . . ."[5]

To such visions we might add other extraordinary phenomena such as hearing Jesus address us in an audible voice, feeling the touch of his hand on our forehead, and so forth. Such external manifestations might seem exciting and convincing, the kind of thing that could be the culmination of our Christ-experience. Yet such an expectation would prove a costly mistake in our spiritual life. These external manifestations are useless in themselves and do not correspond to the way in which Jesus ordinarily wants to reveal himself.

Jesus' contemporaries saw him, heard his voice,

felt his touch. Did this mean they got to know him? Not necessarily. In fact, for many people Christ's physical closeness proved an obstacle. His neighbors at Nazareth, thinking they knew him well, refused to believe in him (Mt 13:53-58). The scribes at Jerusalem rejected him because he was so obviously a Galilean (Jn 7:52). Being allowed to observe Jesus' humanity from close by was a privilege, of course, but it was in no way decisive. What mattered at all times, whether during Jesus' public life or after his resurrection, was acceptance of his word and response to his Spirit. In this regard even his mother, Mary, who was closer to Jesus than any other human person, proved no exception. To the woman who exclaimed, "How happy is the woman who bore you and nursed you!", Jesus replied, "Rather, how happy are those who hear the word of God and obey it!" (Lk 11:27-28). One could only get to know Jesus by opening the mind and heart to his message.

The same applies to external visions and locutions. It may have been a great experience for Ignatius to see Christ as a white figure, but it can hardly have been what moved and convinced him. Rather it was the force of Jesus' word and the work of the Spirit in his heart that made him aware of Jesus' presence. Certainly visual images can be a help. But it really makes very little difference whether it is a photograph of Jesus (if we had any), a vision seen with the eyes of the mind, or an artistic representation. Indeed, an artistic picture may prove a better aid in focusing attention on essentials and diminishing the chance of self-delusion. It is, no doubt, with good reason that Jesus did not leave us a photographic image of his face!

The Spirit Who Comforts

In the above sections I have spoken about Jesus' Spirit. This could easily be understood in general terms. When we speak of someone's spirit, we usually refer to the person's attitudes, approach to life, way of doing things, frame of mind. In this way, speaking of a community we might say, "There is a good spirit here," or of an individual, "She is a spirited person." This was no doubt part of what Jesus intended. But was it all?

In the context of his long discussion at the Last Supper as to how he was to remain present to his disciples, Christ spoke of the Holy Spirit as a new person, another agent to be reckoned with:

"I have said this to you while I am still with you.
But the Paraclete, the Holy Spirit
that the Father will send in my name,
will teach you everything
and remind you of all that I told you" (Jn 14:25-26,AB).

We are not surprised to find the two elements by which Jesus will be present in the future, namely his teaching and the Spirit. This is entirely consistent with what we have seen before. What is startling and new is Jesus' speaking of the Spirit as a person. He will be sent by the Father. He will teach and remind. Was this a metaphorical way of speaking? Did he mean it literally?

When we compare our text with the other Paraclete passages (Jn 14:15-17, 15:26-27 and 16:7-15), it is clear that Jesus is literally referring to a divine person. This person is *another* paraclete or intercessor (Jn 14:16), Jesus himself being the first paraclete (1 Jn 2:1). The new paraclete can come and go, explain, guide, speak and do everything a person can do. More remarkable still is that everything that is said about the Holy Spirit is parallel to whatever the gospel says of Jesus.

The Holy Spirit, like Jesus, comes forth from the Father, is sent by the Father and comes into the world. Jesus is the way, the truth and the life; he is the Spirit of truth, guiding the disciple along the way and giving life. As Jesus will remain with the disciples, so will the Paraclete. As Jesus has often stressed that he had everything in common with the Father, so he now seems to stress that the Spirit has everything in common with him. The Holy Spirit is presented as the "alter ego" of Jesus, as his perfect parallel.[6]

I know that the sameness and separateness of Jesus and the Holy Spirit as described in these passages are employed by theologians to illustrate the doctrine of the Blessed Trinity. The Holy Spirit is, no doubt, a distinct divine person. But dogmatic formulation should not just now distract us from our interest in what the gospel teaches about experiencing God. The Holy Spirit is one way in which we meet God. We can only meet him in this manner after Jesus' death and resurrection.

> "It is for your own good that I go away.
> For if I do not go away,
> the Paraclete will never come to you" (Jn 16:7,AB).

The Holy Spirit, though acting as a person in his own right, will at all times present himself as *Jesus'* Spirit. The Holy Spirit will not bring a new teaching; he will endorse and complete Jesus' word (Jn 14:26). Even if he seems to go beyond what Jesus said, he will never speak on his own, but will only say what he heard from Jesus (as Jesus himself only spoke whatever the Father had commanded him, Jn 16:13-15). Experiencing the presence of the Holy Spirit, we are in fact experiencing the presence of Jesus. Also in this way it is confirmed that Jesus remains with us by his word and his Spirit.

Summing up

Let us conclude this chapter by summarizing briefly some questions we have discussed.

What is the difference, if any, between experiencing Jesus and experiencing God in general? Is there anything distinctive in Christian experience above and beyond the general experience of God?

Yes there is something distinctive in the Christian's experience. Christians receive a specific and clear invitation to life through Jesus' word. Whereas in the general experience of God we become aware of his presence as our Master, as the ultimate meaning for our existence, and so forth, in Jesus Christ we meet God in a more direct and outspoken fashion. Through Jesus we know that, despite all appearances to the contrary, God is love and that our own lives are made meaningful by love.

In what way does Jesus reveal himself to us? What does the experience of Jesus look like in everyday terms? Can it be described in plain, everyday language?

We experience Jesus when we accept his word. This word comes to us through his teaching as left us in the gospels, but also in the sacramental realities of the church. This acceptance becomes a *subjective experience* when we allow ourselves to be carried along by his Spirit who is guiding us interiorly. By the combination of his word and his Spirit, we get to know and love Jesus intimately. By an awareness of what is happening in us, we know that it is Jesus who is doing these things in us.

Are the experiences of God in general (as exemplified in pagan mystics) and the experience of Jesus (as witnessed to by the early Christians) two different experiences? Or are they basically stages of one and the same experience?

They are basically one and the same experience. Experience of God is an awareness of his presence. In the general experience of God, such as found with mystics of other religions, there is an initial awareness of God, the level of awareness possible to man before revelation. Through the

Experiencing Jesus

coming of Jesus, God has become more clearly known; his purpose is more definite. Our general awareness of God can, therefore, become more specific, can be focused better on account of Jesus' word. But it is not a different awareness; it is the same awareness raised to a higher level.

Is there a difference in our experience of the Father, the Son and the Holy Spirit? Do we experience these three Divine Persons in three distinct ways, or do we experience them all by a general awareness?

Theologians have argued about this question for centuries. Simply speaking, the three Divine Persons are only distinct by their mutual relationships, not by anything they do to creatures. Both creation and redemption are the work of all three Persons combined, of God the totality. On the other hand, we know the Blessed Trinity as a trinity precisely because of different manifestations: All beginnings, such as creation and salvation itself, are seen by scripture as springing from the Father; the incarnation is ascribed to the Son; building up the church to the Spirit. I would, therefore, tentatively put forward the opinion that within the same, overall awareness of God's presence in our life, we can be aware of the different ways in which the Persons influence us. There may be a lot of human thinking and subjective feeling in the matter, yet this approach may lead us to a fuller experience of God. We might see the Father at work in those aspects of our experience springing from an openness to existence and nature. We might feel more in contact with the Son when dealing with his word. We might feel close to the Spirit when experiencing his dynamic action in Christ's community or in our own soul. But all these are only shades of the same fundamental experience. Ultimately we know that the Spirit is *Jesus'* Spirit, and that he who sees Jesus, sees the Father.

Jesus' Word and Jesus' Spirit

Three
Scripture and Radiance

In the first chapter we saw that Christ's promise to make himself known to us required as a condition that we keep his word.

> "If anyone loves me,
> he will keep my word.
> Then my Father will love him
> and we shall come to him
> and make our dwelling place with him" (Jn 14:23,AB).

In Chapter 2 we learned that Jesus is present to us through his word and his Spirit. What is Jesus' word? Where do we find it today? How will it help us experience his presence?

Christ's word reaches us in a number of ways. He instructs us through the word of priests and teachers speaking in his name. He heals and nourishes us through the sacramental word. He encourages and guides us through the words of friends. But, although these are all genuine forms of Jesus speaking to us, they all presuppose the original, historical message spoken by Jesus when he was on earth. The actual words uttered by the incarnate Son of God will always remain the source and inspiration of what he says through his Spirit and his church in later ages. The teaching of the Word made flesh may never be forgotten.

It is not difficult to prove this from the gospels. Rather than presenting a long argument, I propose to list here some of the statements regarding his word. Throughout, I render certain synonyms found in scripture—for example, message, truth, teaching—by the English term "words," because it is clear in scripture that these synonyms refer indiscriminately to the overall message of Jesus. For simplicity's sake I have also written them in simple, declarative sentences.

I have the words of eternal life.
My words are truth.

The words I speak come from my Father.
My words are life and spirit.
The words I speak will judge you.

Listen to my words.
Hear my words and believe.
Believe my words.
Believe the words I speak.
Believe because of my words.

Accept my words.
Obey my words.
Try to understand my words.
Recall the words I spoke to you.
Keep my words in your heart.
Allow my words to live in you.
Remain loyal to my words.

Do not be ashamed of me or my words.
Watch over my words like a treasure.
Heaven and earth shall pass away,
    my words shall never pass away.[1]

Jesus tells us that we should take note of his actual words, try to understand them, accept them in faith, treasure them in our hearts and put them into practice. The church, and every Christian for that matter, will always have to return to the actual words of Jesus. I don't mean this in a formalistic or narrow sense. Jesus spoke in Aramaic and the Aramaic idiom, obviously, is not of the essence. Many of Jesus' statements were prophetic and exemplary in purpose; they may never be taken as dogmatic propositions. Nothing would be further from Jesus' mind than wanting his words followed in a fundamentalistic, literalistic manner. Yet, precisely because the Word became flesh and spoke human language, his actual words should always remain the vehicle of contact with future generations. This is why the gospels, why the whole of scripture, is so important for our Christian experience of God.

From "Word" to "Scripture"

The word of Jesus is Sacred Scripture. This may seem a bold assertion. At first sight there might appear to be a vast distance between the sermons Jesus preached in Palestine and our present New Testament. Are we allowed to equate his spoken message with texts that were committed to writing many years afterward?

To do justice to this question, we have to remember how the New Testament arose. We have already seen in Chapter 2 that Jesus taught as a rabbi. He taught his disciples parables and instructions they had to learn by heart. The gospel mentions repeatedly that Jesus did not do all the preaching alone. "Then he sent them out to preach the Kingdom of God" (Lk 9:2). "After this the Lord chose another seventy-two men and sent them out two by two" (Lk 10:1). Since Jesus' disciples were not expected to preach their own message, but Jesus' word, Jesus must have prepared them for this task by providing rather exact formulations of his message. When the disciples went out, they did so armed with a stock of preaching material: parables and comparisons, prophecies and revelations of Jesus, summaries of Jesus' debates with the Pharisees, accounts of Jesus' signs. Even before the resurrection, Jesus' preaching had been given a definite form in a collection of oral traditions.[2]

After Jesus' resurrection his words and deeds were seen in a new perspective. To the earlier traditions were added accounts of his passion and Easter appearances. With the need of instructing ever more catechumens, further explanations and additions arose. Teachers started grouping different elements of the traditions in handy collections: strings of miracles; parables; instructions for various groups; sayings referring to the same topic, such as persecution,[3] etc. Whereas Jews were used to learning things by heart, non-Jews were not, and so there was a tendency to write down the traditions as soon as they were translated into Greek. At a later stage, in different parts of the early church the need was felt for an integrated presentation of Jesus, his work and his teaching. The outcome was the four gospels, four harmonious interpretations based on the oral traditions and written collections. The meaning of Jesus' teaching was further worked out in letters written by the apostles to the early communities and in books such as the Acts of the Apostles and Revelation.

The word developed from oral teaching to written text, from simple record to theological interpretation, from loose traditions to an integrated presentation. Such a development was dictated by the growth and expansion of the church. It was unavoidable. In fact, it was a process of the "maturing" of the word, intended by Christ himself. "I have much more to tell you, but now it would be too much for you to bear. When, however, the Spirit comes, who reveals the truth about God, he will lead you into all the truth" (Jn 16:12-13). The word of Jesus *could not* be fully understood before the resurrection. The church needed the experience of Easter and the awareness of its role in the world for an adequate appreciation of the word of Jesus. The New Testament does not only contain "words" of Jesus in direct quotations attributed to him; it is in its totality a fuller, matured expression of Jesus' word.

There is more. As Karl Rahner has pointed out, the church of apostolic times had the duty of expressing her faith as a lasting norm for the future. This expression of faith resulted in scripture. By founding an apostolic church, God called forth the inspired word that was to remain a constitutive element of the church of all time to come. Or, to put it differently, the apostolic church had the task not merely of preaching the word of Jesus, but of enshrining it in an adequate and lasting written testimony. The New Testament is the word of Jesus laid down as the foundation of the Christian community.[4]

The Old Testament too is related to Jesus' word. The Old Testament was inspired with a view to preparing the way for Jesus. In a certain sense the Old Testament was completed only when the New Testament came about. It received its full meaning from Jesus' word. Jesus' word sealed the Old Testament and the apostolic church acknowledged it as its own prehistory. The Old Testament, too, is an extension of the word of Jesus: It is the past in which it is rooted.[5]

There are many ways in which the word of Jesus can come to us. However, the chief and principal manner in which it has been preserved for us is Sacred Scripture. Scripture enshrines the message Jesus spoke. If we want to hear his word, we cannot afford to neglect scripture. St. Jerome was quite right when he stated: "Ignorance of Scripture means ignorance of Christ."

The Seed and the Fruit

In Section 2 of this book—when narrating the experience of the saints—I will describe specific ways in which Sacred Scripture can form a starting point for meetings with Christ. Here I would like to discuss a more general question. Quite a few Christians today think the Bible is hardly necessary or useful in practical life. Rather than wasting time reading scripture, they maintain, we should be involved in contemporary problems. The Christian should go out to meet Christ in the hungry, the naked and the oppressed. The test of Christian faith is not our fidelity to reading scripture, but our commitment to promoting the welfare and happiness of others.

There are valid points in these remarks. It is deeds that count, not words. Religious practices, including bible reading, may cover up an attempt to escape from real involvement and commitment. On the other hand, the opposite is equally true. Preoccupation with work and activity may disguise an inability or unwillingness to face deep religious questions. The search for a personal encounter with God is at times abandoned under the pretext of working in his name.

What did Jesus himself say about the relationship of his word to activity and involvement? He compared the word to seed, Christian commitment to its fruit. In the parable of the sower he described what may happen to the seed: It may be eaten by birds, it may fall on rocky ground, it may be stifled by thistles, or it may take root in fertile soil. The success of the whole operation depends on circumstances and the disposition of the receivers. But the whole process is begun, is made possible, by God's word. "The sower sows God's message" (Mk 4:14). "The seed is the word of God" (Lk 8:11). The seed is not sown for its own sake; its only purpose is to produce a harvest. But there will be no harvest without seed.

Christ wants us to live committed Christian lives, lives that translate his laws of charity into practice. "My Father's glory is shown by your bearing much fruit" (Jn 15:8). However, such fruit cannot be produced unless we remain firmly attached to Jesus. "A branch cannot bear fruit by itself; it can do so only if it remains in the vine. In the same way you cannot bear fruit unless you remain in me" (Jn 15:4). We can only remain in Jesus, however, if "my words remain in you" (Jn 15:7). In this allegory of the vine and the branches, Jesus' words are like the sap that flows into the branches so that they may bring forth grapes. Particularly interesting in Jesus' words is the connection between "remaining in his word" and "giving glory to the Father." For knowing God's glory is the essence of the New Testament.

> The God who said, "Out of darkness the light shall shine!" is the same God who has made his light shine in our hearts, to bring us the knowledge of God's glory shining in the face of Christ (2 Cor 4:6).

The essence of our Christian life is a new light which God creates in our hearts. God himself *is* light. He reveals his inner nature by the radiance of his love. This light, this love, radiates especially from the face of Christ who is the perfect revelation of the Father. As God began our existence with a creative word, "Let there be light," so Jesus initiates our life as adopted children of God by his message of love. The light which God creates in the heart of the Christian makes him *know*—that is, experience—God's radiance as it shines in the face of Christ.

God's Radiance[6]

The word for "glory" in Greek is *doxa,* which is itself the Septuagint equivalent of Hebrew *kabôd.* In the New Testament *doxa* is never used with the ordinary Greek meaning of "opinion." It always follows the specific scriptural meanings given to it by Old Testament usage. The original meaning of *kabôd* is "heaviness," in the sense of importance, of having weight and momentum. When applied to God it indicates that quality by which God communicates his greatness to us by showing us his mighty deeds.

> It implies that which makes God impressive to man, the force of his self-manifestation. As everywhere attested in the Old Testament, God is intrinsically invisible. Nevertheless, when he reveals himself, e.g., in meteorological phenomena, one may rightly speak of

the *kabôd* of Yahweh, of the manifestation that makes on man a highly significant impression.[7]

In English, *kabôd* has generally been translated as "glory." I prefer to render it as "radiance"—and have done so in the bible quotations remaining in this chapter (see italized words)—partly because this term is more meaningful in our own day than the bookish expression "glory" and partly because "radiance" corresponds more closely to the scriptural concept.

> The nature of the *kabôd* itself (as seen in Ex 40:34-35) is to be conceived as a radiant, fiery substance. There proceeds from it fire which consumes the awaiting sacrifice, and after speaking with God, Moses has a radiance of countenance which dazzles the Israelites.[8]

Ezekiel gives a description in his opening vision. God himself came in a storm "with brightness round about it, and fire flashing forth continually" (Ez 1:4,RSV). He was surrounded by cherubim and seated on a chariot. God himself was only seen indirectly, as a brilliant, luminous silhouette in human shape.

> High up on the throne was a being that looked like a man. I saw him shine like bronze, and close to and all around him from what seemed his loins upwards was what looked like fire; and from what seemed his loins downwards I saw what looked like fire, and a light all round like a bow in the clouds on rainy days; that is how the surrounding light appeared. It was something that looked like the *radiance* of Yahweh (Ez 1:26b-28b,JB).

God's radiance is visible in the created world (Is 6:3; Ps 57:5). But God's radiance is manifested particularly by his saving deeds:

> "So shall I *show a radiance* at the expense of Pharaoh, of all his army, his chariots, his horsemen" (Ex 14:17,JB).

> "Yahweh I sing: he has covered himself in *radiance,* horse and rider he has thrown into the sea" (Ex 15:1,JB).

Also the new exodus announced by Deutero-Isaiah will manifest God's radiance:

> "Then the *radiance* of the LORD will be revealed,
> and all mankind will see it" (Is 40:5).

The mightiest manifestation of God's radiance is the exaltation of the Risen Christ:

> He was made visible in the flesh,
> attested by the Spirit,
> seen by angels,
> proclaimed to the pagans,
> believed in by the world,
> taken up *with radiance* (1 Tm 3:16,JB).

Stephen saw *"the radiance of God* and Jesus standing at the right side of God" (Acts 7:55). The exaltation of Christ will be completed at the Last Judgment, "when the *radiance* of our great God and Savior Jesus Christ will appear" (Ti 2:13). At his transfiguration, Jesus gave to the three apostles an anticipated view of the radiance he was to possess. "They woke up and saw Jesus' *radiance"* (Lk 9:32).

Radiance and the Effect of God's Word

In the Old Testament, God's radiance was understood to be a manifestation of the divine majesty. We need not be surprised that, generally speaking, human beings could not be said to partake of the divine radiance. Men and women may *see* God's radiance (Is 35:2, 66:18); they cannot share it.

A notable exception was what had happened to Moses. This need not surprise us. Moses was considered exceptional for many reasons. It was he who mediated the covenant at Sinai that would change Israel's history forever. It was Moses who performed miracles and wonders that surpassed those of all other prophets. But, most of all, Moses was known to be exceptional on account of his close familiarity with God. "There has never been a prophet in Israel like

Moses; the LORD spoke with him face-to-face" (Dt 34:10). If someone has experienced God in such an intimate way, what is more natural than that the effects can be observed?

When God appeared to Moses in the beginning, he showed himself "in the shape of a flame of fire, coming from the middle of a bush" (Ex 3:2,JB). Even at that early stage Moses was overcome by God's presence. He put off his shoes, covered his face, and listened to God's word with his forehead touching the ground. But on Mount Sinai he was even closer to God. When he requested, "Show me your *radiance*" (Ex 33:18,JB), God showed him a glimpse of himself. God's radiance passed by him and God spoke infinitely tender words: "I, the LORD, am a God who is full of compassion and pity, who is not easily angered and who shows great love and faithfulness" (Ex 34:6). God stood near Moses and pronounced his own name, "Yahweh." Again Moses responded by worshiping God, face to the ground.

"When Moses went down from Mount Sinai carrying the Ten Commandments, his face was shining because he had been speaking with the LORD; but he did not know it" (Ex 34:29). The people were frightened by the radiance on his face. They did not dare to approach him. For this reason, Moses had to cover his face with a veil. He took the veil off only when entering the tent of the Lord's presence to speak to God. "When he came out, he would tell the people of Israel everything that he had been commanded to say, and they would see that his face was shining. Then he would put the veil back on until the next time he went to speak to the LORD" (Ex 34:34-35). Because Moses was full of God's presence and carrying his word, he shared in his radiance.

St. Paul takes up this example from the Old Testament to illustrate what happens to us through our contact with Christ. God's speaking to Moses was visible on his face; so too Jesus' speaking to us in the Spirit is visible in us. In the Old Testament God's word was still restricted, it was to some extent a "dead" word, a written text; in the New Testament Christ gave us a living word, a word constantly made relevant through his Spirit. The following passage should be carefully read. The last verse quoted is especially important.

> The Law was carved in letters on stone tablets, and God's *radiance* appeared when it was given. Even though the brightness on Moses' face was fading, it was so strong that the people of Israel could not keep their eyes fixed on him. If the Law, which brings death when it is in force, came with such *radiance*, how much greater is the *radiance* that belongs to the activity of the Spirit! The system which brings condemnation was *radiant;* how much more *radiant* is the activity which brings salvation! We may say that because of the far brighter *radiance* now the *radiance* that was so bright in the past is gone. For if there was *radiance* in that which lasted for a while, how much more *radiance* is there in that which lasts forever!
>
> Because we have this hope, we are very bold. We are not like Moses, who had to put a veil over his face so that the people of Israel would not see the brightness fade and disappear. Their minds, indeed, were closed; and to this very day their minds are covered with the same veil as they read the books of the old covenant. The veil is removed only when a person is joined to Christ. Even today, whenever they read the Law of Moses, the veil still covers their minds. But it can be removed, as the scripture says about Moses: "His veil was removed when he turned to the Lord." Now, "the Lord" in this passage is the Spirit; and where the Spirit of the Lord is present, there is freedom. All of us, then, reflect the *radiance* of the Lord with uncovered faces; and that same *radiance*, coming from the Lord, who is the Spirit, transforms us into his likeness in an ever greater degree of *radiance* (2 Cor 3:7-18).

This is, indeed, a bold statement. Paul claims that

God speaks to us, as he did to Moses, face to face, and that this makes our lives radiant. Christ speaks through his word and his Spirit. We are transformed by it into an ever greater likeness of Christ. The word of God kindles a fire in our heart that shines through in our words and deeds. The inner experience of Christ's presence changes our personality.

> The God who said, "Out of darkness the light shall shine!" is the same God who made his light shine in our hearts, to bring us to the knowledge of God's *radiance* shining in the face of Christ (2 Cor 4:6).

What Scripture Should Do

From this chapter we may be able to piece together a rather complete picture of what the study of scripture means in our lives.

To remain in touch with Jesus we have to absorb scripture. Scripture contains that word which Jesus so earnestly commanded us to hear, to remember and to put into practice. By meditating on scripture we make it possible for Jesus to work in us and transform our lives.

Even though the word is contained in the written text of the Old and New Testaments, it is not a dead or static entity. Rather it is like a seed. It contains life. It can grow. A word spoken by Jesus, sown in our heart, can become the starting point of a new commitment, a new kind of life.

The word is the life-giving sap by which Jesus nourishes our interior life. Together with the sacramental graces he imparts, Jesus keeps us strong and fresh with the words he addresses to us. Thus we can produce fruits, the acts of selfless love and charity that prove us to be his disciples.

Jesus' word kindles a light in our hearts. This light

makes us aware of his presence, aware also of the activity of his Spirit in us. Jesus' light shines from within us. Gradually it transforms us into his likeness so that Jesus' presence in us becomes visible in what we say and do.

Reflection on scripture is not the study of an ancient text, a struggle with concepts and words. Rather it should be a living encounter with Christ whom we meet in his word and his Spirit. The written text is no more than a seed or a spark. In the radiance and the fire that ensue, the Spirit takes over.

Conclusion

Our starting point was Jesus' promise:

"Whoever keeps the commandments that he has from
    me
is the man who loves me;
and the man who loves me will be loved by my Father,
and I shall love him
and reveal myself to him" (Jn 14:21,AB).

We may now be in a position to appreciate the full meaning of these words:

Jesus promised he would give us
a real experience of himself.

He will manifest himself
so that we know
his love
and his living presence
in us.

To receive this gift
we need
to accept his words,
absorb them,
put them into practice.

If we show our love in this way,
he will fill us abundantly
with his Spirit
with his love.

We will radiate Christ
in our lives.
We will know him
with a knowledge
enkindled by love.

Section II
Saints and Mystics Show the Way

Four

Symeon the New Theologian

It was the year 998 in Constantinople. The Patriarch
Sisinnios presided over a meeting of theologians in one
of the well-furnished halls of his palace. Those were
the days when speculative thinking flourished in the
Orthodox Church, with all its ornate oratory, its
hairsplitting definitions of terms and subtle reasoning.
Some famous men attended the meeting.

Stephen of Nicomedia took the floor. He was the
Patriarch's own theologian. The status and influence of
this function can be judged from the fact that Stephen
had resigned an archbishopric to take it up. With all the
weight of his authority, Stephen launched a full-scale
attack on the monk Symeon who was also present:

> "What are these strange teachings we all hear
> about, Symeon Abbot of Mamas?! The whole of Con-
> stantinople resounds with your bizarre assertions! Do
> you pretend to be a theologian? Where, tell me, did you
> make your studies? What learned men were your
> teachers? You are ignorant of professional theology!
> How can you presume to speak about things that lie
> beyond your competence? Stop preaching and writing,
> remain silent before learned men! Or otherwise prove
> to us now that you are a theologian. Tell us here in this
> assembly: within the Blessed Trinity how do you dis-
> tinguish between Father and Son? Do you maintain a
> real or a rational distinction?"

Symeon replied:

> "You, theologians, are wasting your time by your
> endless speculations about useless questions. Your
> highfaluting language and your clever arguments do not
> bring you nearer to God.
>
> God the Son sent his Holy Spirit, but not to

orators, not to philosophers, not to those who read many books, not to those who give themselves or others titles, not to men who seek influence and fame. No, he sends his Spirit to those who are humble in mentality and in their way of living, to persons who speak simply, who live more simply and whose thinking is simpler still. Such persons will be taught by the Holy Spirit himself. They have no need of human learning. Enlightened by the Spirit they look at the Son, they see the Father and adore the Trinity of Persons.

What use is discussion about God if you are not consciously aware of his presence? What value have theoretical distinctions between the Divine Persons if we do not know the difference between them by experience? You are blind men talking about the type of metal a coin is made of while you are unable to see the coin itself! You have not felt the Divine Light within your hearts, yet you dare to discuss the intricate mysteries of the Trinity! You quote Scripture but remain unaware of its intrinsic meaning. Only persons filled with the Holy Spirit, only those taught by God himself, can teach theology to others."[1]

The incident was more than a clash of personalities. With Symeon, the New Theologian, as he was to become known, experiential theology reasserted itself in the face of predominantly academic scholarship. A system based on cold and abstract speculations was being threatened by the appeal to charismatic norms. Although Symeon if properly understood never proclaimed any heresy, he was accused and persecuted till his death.[2]

Scripture in a New Light

The attacks of established theologians on Symeon's learning were hardly deserved. Symeon was an erudite man. He had probably read and digested more than many of his contemporaries. Even as a young man moving freely in the well-to-do families of Constantinople, Symeon had studied scripture and the writings of the Fathers under the guidance of personal tutors. When he entered the monastery at the age of 27 (in the year 976), he was so well prepared that he could be ordained a priest a year later and become Abbot of Mamas within four years. The reason why Symeon became unpopular with the theological establishment was exactly the opposite of being deficient in learning: He knew his Christian sources so well that he could strike out in a new direction.

In Symeon's day the whole life of a Christian had become dominated by tradition. As Christian faith was officially adhered to by all, its assimilation in teaching and preaching had become a matter of routine. Believing was no longer a personal conquest of truth; it had become part of imbibing the local culture. External liturgy flourished, but real prayer had little chance to develop. Worship had deteriorated into a complicated ritual of which every bow and every formula was carefully prescribed; it was too smooth to appeal to a person wrestling with his living God.

Symeon put his finger on the sore spot when he pointed out that the experiential side of religion was lacking. He found too many glib assertions in theology, too much externalism in prayer, too much dependence on the *"ex-opere-operato"* working of the sacraments. By all this the heart of Christianity was lost. Believing in Christ means a living encounter with him, a discovery of the Holy Spirit in one's life, a growth in personal love for the three Persons of the Blessed Trinity.

This, Symeon saw, was what Christ spoke about in the gospels. In his high-priestly prayer Christ had prayed to the Father, "May they be in us, just as you are in me and I am in you" (Jn 17:21). But surely the Father and the Son are united in a very personal and conscious union! If Jesus says that we are to be in the Father and the Son as the Father is in the Son and the Son in the Father, doesn't he state that we too will share in a personal and loving communion? It is obvious from Jesus' words that this communion should start on earth. It follows that even here on earth we shall participate in the intimate knowledge Father and Son have of one another.

Jesus said that whoever sees him sees his Father (Jn 14:7). Seeing is important in life. We cannot speak adequately of what we have not seen. And we cannot speak about God unless we have seen him. Jesus promised that we would "see" him. It is the kind of seeing that reveals to us his divinity, his relationship with the Father. Jesus did not mean seeing in a physical sense, otherwise those who crucified him would have seen the Father!

Jesus had exclaimed, "Who is my mother? . . . Whoever does what my Father in heaven wants him to do is . . . my mother!" (Mt 12:48-50). Yes, Symeon said, when we become Christians we conceived Christ. Christ is born in us not corporeally, as in Mary the Mother of God, but in a spiritual sense. We become like a woman carrying a child. But surely we should then become aware of this divine life moving in us just as a pregnant woman becomes aware that new life stirs within her!

Jesus came "to set the earth on fire" (Lk 12:49). Jesus was referring to the fire of the Holy Spirit which he would infuse into our souls. If this is so, Symeon argues, it cannot happen in an invisible and unconscious manner. For the essence of the soul is knowing and feeling. It must notice the divine flame that soars up in itself and consumes everything.

Paul tells us that we have put on Christ (Gal 3:27). Whoever puts on clothes, knows what he is doing. A Christian worthy of the name has put on Christ consciously and knowingly. As he feels his clothes with his naked body, so he is aware of Christ acting upon him. Only a corpse feels nothing. Likewise a Christian who is "dead" is unaware of Christ's presence within.

The more Symeon studied scripture, the more confirmation he found for believing that a Christian should be able to experience Christ in a conscious manner. Without denying the validity of external rites and sacraments, Symeon set his heart on proclaiming again the inner, spiritual principle of Christian life. A Christian lives in Christ, has become bone of his bone and flesh of his flesh (Eph 5:30). But it is a true communion only if we are aware of it!

Baptism of the Spirit

More than any other theologian before or after him, Symeon put conscious awareness of Christ at the center of Christian doctrine. For him, knowing God in a direct way is no luxury, nor a privilege reserved to a select few. The following statements speak for themselves:

> Whoever is known by God, knows he is known and knows that he sees God.
>
> God shows himself openly and makes himself known very consciously.
>
> The Son of God, God himself, has come to earth to reunite us to himself consciously through his Spirit.
>
> The greatest misfortune that can befall a Christian is not to know consciously that God lives within him.
>
> Persons who do not realize God's presence in a conscious way, have no right to be called spiritual.[3]

When a child is baptized, grace is given and the Blessed Trinity make their indwelling. Yet for full Christian maturity this is not enough. The growing child should become more and more aware of the Three Persons acting within him or her. Becoming consciously aware of this divine action is another kind of baptism, a "baptism in the Holy Spirit." Symeon points out that scripture too distinguishes such a baptism of the Spirit from sacramental baptism. Cornelius and his family were baptized in the Holy Spirit even before they were baptized with water (Acts 10:44-48). Baptism in the Holy Spirit can and should be experienced by every Christian.

> Be fully assured that even here below the sealing by the Holy Spirit will be given to us in a conscious manner.
> God gives us the same certitude that he gave to the apostles, thanks to his giving us the abiding presence of the Holy Spirit.
> If the Holy Spirit is in you, you cannot fail to notice his action within you.
> Those who do not possess the Spirit as one who acts and speaks in them, cannot be reckoned to be "faithful."[4]

Symeon's Own Experience

People often objected to Symeon: "What you talk about no one has ever experienced!" To meet this objection, Symeon would talk about his own inner spiritual life. He would supplement his theological teaching with reports of what he had seen happening to others or to himself. His instructions and hymns thus afford us valuable insights into the experiences of a genuine mystic.

Symeon speaks of two forms of awareness: moments of ecstasy which occur rarely; a state of awareness that remains with us all the time. The abiding state can be recognized by feelings of peace and joy, by surrendering to the gentle inspirations of the Holy Spirit, by a subtle persuasion of God's all-pervasive presence. This state of general awareness is strengthened and clarified by the peak experiences we have during ecstatic prayer.

Symeon left us clear descriptions of what happened to him during such peak experiences. He called them visions of light. Symeon had been struck by the fact that scripture often uses images derived from light.

God is light (1 Jn 1:5).
"I am the light of the world" (Jn 8:12).
"Wake up, sleeper,
    and rise from death
and Christ will shine on you" (Eph 5:14).
How can light and darkness live together? (2 Cor 6:14).

Symeon was fond of these metaphors because he too had seen God as a light, not an external, visible light, but a light that illumined the mind.

When trying to explain this light, Symeon is often at a loss for words. Perhaps what he is saying could be paraphrased in the following way. When at prayer he would occasionally become distinctly aware of Christ as a light surrounding him on all sides. This light was not something that he could see with his bodily eyes; it had no shape, no form, no precise image. Rather, he felt a sensation in his mind of enlargement, of space, of radiance, of weightlessness and joy, a sensation that could best be expressed by "seeing an inner light." The reality of it was overwhelming; the "how," difficult to understand or to express in words.

Symeon says he is convinced that many beginners are granted visions of this light, but they lose them by not being sensitive to them. Becoming aware of Christ's light in such an unspeakable fashion requires adopting the frame of mind Jesus prescribed in the gospel. Only the humble, the poor in spirit, those who hunger and thirst for God, those who are pure of heart, will see Christ clearly. Unfortunately, many Christians fall short of these requirements; few develop their spiritual eyes to the full. In one realistic passage Symeon laments that, although every Christian could partake of the divine light in a conscious manner, "only one in a thousand, no, one in ten thousand" arrives at mystical contemplation.

Light in the Midst of Darkness

I can conclude this sketch of Symeon in no better way than by reproducing here his own account of a vision. The text is a free translation of Hymn 25:1-66. In this unique testimony we get a rare glimpse of what a true mystic experienced. We see how from meditating on scripture he passed into ecstasy and what prayers came to his mind. Although it may seem extraordinary at first sight, further consideration of the details will bring the realization that the whole event lies within the scope of every praying Christian. Leaving personal differences aside, what Symeon described could be our own experience.

> Master, I saw your face, how shall I describe it?
> I looked upon your beauty, how shall I speak of what is
> unspeakable. . . .
>
> I was sitting in the light of a lamp.
> Its light shone on me, it lit up the darkness and the
> shadow of night.
> I was reading in the light of the lamp,
> reflecting on words, examining statements.
> Then, Master, as I was meditating on these things,
> suddenly you appeared from above,
> much larger than the sun.
> As a ray of brilliant light you shone from heaven into
> my heart.
>
> Everything else I saw as shadow.
> Except that in the middle there was a column of light
> that cut through the air
> passing from heaven down to me. . . .
>
> At once I forgot the light of the lamp.
> I was no longer aware of being inside the house.
> I seemed to sit surrounded by darkness.
> I lost contact with my body.
> But I said to you and I say it again from the bottom of
> my heart:
> "Have mercy on me, Master
> have mercy on me, my All. . . ."

Experiencing Jesus

But oh what intoxication of light,
oh what movements of fire!
Oh what swirlings of the flame in me
coming from you and your glory!
And all this in spite of my nothingness!

I recognize the glory.
I know it is your Holy Spirit,
who shares the same nature with you, who shares your
    honor,
O Word!

He possesses the same kinship, the same glory, the
    same essence,
he alone with your Father and with you, O Christ,
Oh God of the universe!

In adoration I fall down before you.
I thank you for making me experience the power of
    your divinity,
however small this experience may have been.
I thank you for revealing yourself to me.
Though I was sitting in darkness, you enlightened me.
You granted me to see the light of your face,
a light no man can endure.

I know I was sitting in the middle of darkness,
but while I was there surrounded by darkness, you
    appeared as light.
You lit me up completely by your light.
I became light in the night,
I who found myself in total darkness.
The darkness did not extinguish your light,
nor did the light dispel the visible darkness.
The two were together, yet completely separate, with-
    out confusion,
at a distance from each other,
not at all mixed except in the same spot where they
    filled everything
so it seems to me.

I am in the light, though I am in the middle of darkness.
I am in the darkness, yet in the middle of light.

Symeon the New Theologian
69

How can darkness receive within itself a light,
how can it remain in the middle of the light,
without being dissipated by it?

Oh what a marvellous thing I see with my double vision,
with my two sets of eyes,
with the eyes of my body and the eyes of my soul!
What I am talking to you about are the wonderful
mysteries of
a double God, a God who came to me in a twofold
manner.
He took upon himself my human nature
and he gave me his Spirit.
So I too became god by divine grace,
a true son of God but a son by adoption.
Oh what dignity, what glory![5]

Five
Thérèse of Lisieux

A French girl entered a convent at a very young age; she died at 23. This happened on September 30, 1897. Within a few years she was known all over the world. Not quite 28 years later, on May 17, 1925, she was canonized a saint for the universal church. This is the remarkable success story of Marie Françoise Thérèse Martin, daughter of a simple clockmaker, now one of the most popular patron saints, often referred to as "The Little Flower."

Thérèse became known by her autobiography, *The Story of a Soul*, in which she described her life and her religious ideals. It was a rather personal and confidential account, never intended by her for wider circulation. But when it was released after her death, it proved an immediate bestseller. At present it is available in 35 languages and sales are reckoned in millions of copies. What is there in this short, 70,000-word book that it merited such a response?

In fact, reading the book for the first time it may well be that one is appalled. Here, one thinks, is a book such as any schoolgirl might write. Small incidents are blown up as if they were major events. The vocabulary flows over with terms of endearment. Sentiment and emotion abound. But, if one takes the trouble to read on and to read more carefully, one discovers the fallacy of this first impression. Under the undeniable teenage style—and what else can one expect from a French girl, born and bred in a bourgeois family, writing in a romantic period?—one meets a spiritual tough-mindedness that fascinates and inspires.

Thérèse struggled with questions that are still relevant today: What is the purpose of existence? What happens at death? Will there be an afterlife? How can we reconcile human loneliness and smallness with our desire to be great and worthwhile? As Bernard Bro remarked, Thérèse was as radical in facing such questions as her contemporaries Rimbaud, Dostoyevski, Nietzsche, Claudel, Freud and Van Gogh.[1] Thérèse had tasted the reality of death. When she was four years old, her mother died. She witnessed the soul-destroying agony of her father. During her first year in the convent an epidemic of influenza brought five deaths among the sisters. "Death reigned everywhere. No sooner had a sister breathed her last than we had to leave her to look after others."[2]

Thérèse completed the last chapters of her book two months before her death. She had had a premonition of her death. She had been coughing up blood and medical science could do little about it in those days. With horror she stood before the abyss of nothingness that awaits every human being. A mist of doubt and uncertainty engulfed her. "I can't believe anymore in eternal life," she confided to a friend. "It seems to me that after this mortal life nothing will remain. I have lost everything."[3] "I am in a dark tunnel and you would have to go through it yourself to understand how dark it is." At times her whole life seemed an illusion:

> You dream of light and of a fragrant land; you dream that the creator of this loveliness will be your own for all eternity; you dream of escaping one day from these mists in which you languish! Dream on, welcome death; it will not bring you what you hope; it will bring an even darker night, the night of nothingness![4]

In the face of such existential questions, Thérèse knowingly and happily opted for a complete surrender to God in faith. Her book is the candid testimony of a great person, a unique example of how faith can be lived with intensity and depth in a seemingly short and insignificant human life. Small wonder that many people all over the world have recognized their own problems and aspirations in *The Story of a Soul*.

The Influence of Scripture

As I stated before, first impressions are deceptive. This also applies to the way in which Thérèse quoted scripture. The texts she uses are presented in such an easy, offhand manner that we hardly notice what an extraordinary collection they form! Since Thérèse was not writing a scriptural essay and only referred to texts because they had personal meaning for her, their prominence throughout her writing is truly impressive.

The Story of a Soul contains a total of 121 quotations. Almost half are from the gospels (22 in Luke, 18 in John, 16 in Matthew, 2 in Mark). She cites a verse from the psalms 21 times; from St. Paul's letters nine times. Revelation, Exodus, 1 and 2 Kings, Ezekiel, Joel and Ecclesiastes each merit one quotation. But this does not exhaust her Old Testament treasury. Her favorite texts are from Isaiah (7), Canticles (7), Wisdom (5), Proverbs (5), and Tobit (2). If we keep in mind that only five texts are quoted a second time and that Thérèse did not write to impress an audience, the wide range is truly astounding! Clearly her preference went to the gospels, the psalms, Isaiah, Canticles and the Wisdom books.

Thérèse had made scripture her special source book. Repeatedly she testified to having found in it the inspiration and enlightenment she was looking for. Scripture satisfied her where other books failed.

> Sometimes when I read books in which perfection is put before us with the goal obstructed by a thousand obstacles, my poor little head is quickly fatigued. I close the learned treatise which tires my brain and dries up my heart, and I turn to the Sacred Scriptures. Then all becomes clear and full of light.[5]

Thérèse of Lisieux

The works of St. John of the Cross have been such a source of light to me. Between the ages of sixteen and eighteen I read no one else. Later on, spiritual writers always left me cold, and still do. Whenever I open a book, no matter how beautiful or touching, my heart dries up and I can understand nothing of what I read; or if I do understand, my mind will go no further, and I cannot meditate. I am rescued from this helpless state by the Scriptures and the Imitation, finding in them a hidden manna, pure and substantial; but during meditation I am sustained above all else by the Gospels. They supply my poor soul's every need, and they are always yielding up to me new lights and mysterious hidden meanings. I know from experience that "the kingdom of God is within us," that Jesus has no need of books or doctors to instruct our soul; he, the doctor of doctors, teaches us without the sounds of words.[6]

Scripture addresses each person in a different way. In my analysis of what scripture did for Thérèse, I believe that its main function was to supply metaphors which helped her understand herself and her relation to God. Without, perhaps, being aware of it, each one of us has a number of concepts through which we interpret ourselves and the world around us. These "personal constructs" are of great psychological importance: They provide the framework within which we think and act.[7] It is my opinion that Thérèse, like many other people, used metaphors when formulating her constructs and that scripture guided and confirmed her in this.

Take, for example, the metaphor of sailing through life like a ship. It was a natural expression on Thérèse's lips. "I seem to be lost like a little boat without a pilot, at the mercy of the storm-tossed waves."[8] "Instead of the howling wind, a gentle breeze was swelling my sails, and I thought I had already reached harbor."[9] "Tranquil, unruffled by the slightest wind, were the waters on which the little boat was sailing under a sky of cloudless blue."[10] "God launched me full sail upon a sea of confidence and love."[11] Thérèse herself said about the metaphor:

> I remember how often I would say that line from a beautiful poem that father used to recite: "The world is but a ship and not thy home"; these words young as I was encouraged me, and although so many of my childish dreams have faded with the years, the symbol of a ship still charms me and makes my exile easier to bear. Does not the Book of Wisdom say: "Life is like a ship that passeth through the waves: when it is gone, the trace thereof cannot be found."[12]

Here we have a characteristic sample of Thérèse's thinking. A metaphor which she knew from her own experience is further deepened and confirmed by a quotation from scripture.

Thérèse called herself "the little flower." When we read her life story we are not surprised at this. From early childhood flowers meant a lot to her. She tells of the flowers the family used to grow in the garden, of the children collecting daisies in little baskets. She remembers a storm in the field and how "the huge daisies, taller even than I was, were glistening with jewels." She used to weave crowns of daisies and forget-me-nots for the statue of our Lady. During the procession of the Blessed Sacrament she used to be one of the little brides. "Then I could scatter the flowers beneath the feet of God! I used to throw them up high into the air before they fell and when my rose petals touched the monstrance my happiness was complete."[13] When she told her father that she wanted to enter the convent, it was he who explicitly compared her to a flower.

> We went on walking for a long time; my heart grew light again, and father dried his tears, talking to me just like a saint. Going to a low stone wall, he showed me some little white flowers like very small lilies; then he picked one of them, and gave it to me, explaining how carefully God had brought it to blossom, and preserved it

till that day. So striking was the resemblance between the little flower and little Thérèse that it seemed as if I was listening to the story of my own life.[14]

Therefore when Thérèse called herself "the little flower" she did so deliberately, expressing at once her purpose in life and her place in God's plan. "It pleases him to create great saints, who may be compared with the lilies or the rose; but he has also created little ones, who must be content to be daisies or violets nestling at his feet to delight his eyes when he should choose to look at them."[15]

Thérèse acknowledged that the origin of the metaphor was her own experience: "Jesus chose to enlighten me on this mystery. He opened the book of nature before me, and I saw that every flower he has created has a beauty of its own."[16] But she delighted in finding that in the Song of Songs the bride of the beloved is compared to "the flower of the field and the lily of the valley."[17]

There are other metaphors that Thérèse uses. She compares herself to a toy, a plaything with which Jesus may do as he pleases.[18] She is a brush with which Jesus paints; she is a shepherd, a queen.[19] Most of these metaphors were based on her experience; any other person in her stead might have developed them too. But there are other metaphors, quite decisive in Thérèse's spiritual journey, which came to her as an insight from scripture. They were spiritual discoveries that caused her to see herself in a new light. It is this influence of scripture on Thérèse that I would like to trace in a few important examples.

The Way of Childhood

Thérèse's main insight was the recognition that sanctity does not lie in our human efforts and successes, but in allowing God to do his work in us. This was her way of "spiritual childhood." "To remain small means to acknowledge one's own nothingness, to expect all from the good Lord as a small child expects all from his father, not to be worried about anything."[20] Although this may seem simple and straightforward, it was in fact a startling insight.

With her contemporaries, Thérèse strove after greatness. She wanted to make something of her life, to achieve something worthwhile, to do great things for Christ. "I want to be a warrior, a priest, an apostle, a doctor of the Church, a martyr—there is no heroic deed I do not wish to perform. I feel as daring as a crusader, ready to die for the Church upon the battlefield."[21] She understood quite well that she could also make something worthwhile of her life as a contemplative nun, but how could she reach the summit in this vocation? Her weak constitution did not allow severe mortification; time might be too short for many years of slogging at the acquisition of virtue.

The insight she arrived at was almost like a paradox. Greatness in the biblical sense does not lie in external achievements, not even achievements in virtue and spirituality. True greatness consists in becoming like a child, in accepting oneself with all simplicity, in surrendering oneself unconditionally to God's care and love. This wholehearted submission of oneself in poverty of spirit, deceptively easy as it may look, does in reality require a real conversion of heart and heroic strength. But it was a "short cut" to sanctity which, Thérèse felt, was just the thing for her and "little souls" like herself!

In a revealing passage of her autobiography, Thérèse narrates how she discovered this metaphor of "spiritual childhood" which became an important key to her own self-understanding:

> I said to myself: "God would never inspire me with desires which cannot be realized, so in spite of my littleness, I can hope to be a saint. I could never grow up. I must put up with myself as I am, full of imperfec-

tions, but I will find a short cut to heaven, very short and direct, an entirely new way. We live in an age of inventions now, and the wealthy no longer have to take the trouble to climb the stairs; they take a lift. That is what I must find, *a lift* to take me straight up to Jesus, because I am too little to climb the steep stairway of perfection.

"So I searched the Scriptures for some hint of my desired lift until I came upon these words from the lips of eternal wisdom: 'Whosoever is a little one, let him come to me.' I went closer to God feeling sure that I was on the right path, but as I wanted to know what he would do to 'a little one' I continued my search. This is what I found: 'You shall be carried at the breasts and upon the knees; as one whom the mother caresses, so will I comfort you.' My heart had never been moved by such tender and consoling words before!

"Your arms, my Jesus, are the lift which will take me up to heaven. There is no need for me to grow up; on the contrary, I must stay little, and become more and more so. Oh God, you have gone beyond my dreams and I—I only want to sing your mercies!"[22]

In another text Thérèse again refers to this discovery in scripture. She recognizes that it was Jesus himself who revealed his will to her through the sayings of scripture. "Jesus has chosen to show me the only way which leads to the divine furnace of love; it is the way of childlike self-surrender, the way of a child who sleeps, afraid of nothing, in its father's arms." She then enumerates four scripture texts that contain this message: To Proverbs 9:4 and Isaiah 66:12-13, already quoted above, she adds, "To him that is little, mercy is granted" (Wis 6:7) and "The Lord shall feed his flock like a shepherd. . . and shall take them up into his bosom" (Is 40:11). Again she witnesses to her emotion at the discovery of this message. "One can only remain silent, one can only weep for gratitude and love, after words like these. If only every one weak and imperfect like me felt as I do, no one would despair of reaching the heights of love, for Jesus does not ask for glorious deeds. He asks only for self-surrender and for gratitude."[23]

Thérèse was convinced that Jesus himself had spoken to her through these texts. Applying to herself the scriptural metaphor of being "a little one," "a child," she gave a new direction to her spiritual life.

Crying Like a Young Swallow

When Thérèse was small she possessed various birds, among them a canary and a linnet.[24] With her natural tendency to see herself reflected in what happened around her, she must have thought of herself as she saw the birds fluttering in their cage. Writing that the authorities at first refused to allow her to enter the convent on account of her young age, she remarks, "The dove was free to fly to the ark, but the ark refused to let her in."[25] In another text she says, "I long to fly and imitate the eagle, but all I can do is flutter my small wings. I am not strong enough to fly."[26] Although the metaphor came naturally enough to her, it had acquired a special meaning through Thérèse's reflection on scripture.

She writes in passing about a teacher at school who was particularly popular with her classmates. Thérèse says that for some reason or other she herself was not carried away by this particular friendship. She muses that this was a good thing because too intimate a human affection might have drawn her away from God. "I should have been caught easily, and had my wings clipped, and then how could I have 'flown away and been at rest'? How can a heart that is taken up in human love be fully united to God? I am sure that is not possible."[27] The remarkable thing here is the casual way in which Thérèse quoted Psalm 55:6: "I wish I had wings like a dove: I would fly away and find rest!" Surely Thérèse had often repeated this passage to herself because it expressed her desire to fly like a dove and find rest.

A similarly unexpected reference comes in the context of a discussion on her novitiate. Looking back at that time of initiation, Thérèse admitted that she made many mistakes and that God had given her much progress since. "God is certainly very good to have lifted up my soul and lent it wings. The nets of the hunters can no longer frighten me for 'a net is set in vain before the eyes of them that have wings.' "[28] The turn of thought is so unexpected, the connection with the verse quoted so tenuous, that we can only infer that here again Thérèse is quoting a scripture verse she had internalized. Otherwise, Proverbs 1:17 would hardly be the kind of passage one would remember in such a context! No, the image of hunters setting their nets to ensnare unsuspecting birds must have seemed very powerful to her!

The longest elaboration of the metaphor she gives in the last chapter of her book, a chapter she wrote two months before she died. Again quoting an unusual scripture text, Isaiah 38:14, she likens herself to a small, helpless bird: "I cry like a young swallow." And presupposing Deuteronomy 32:11, although she does not quote the text explicitly, she considers Christ to be the eagle which teaches its young to fly. Her own small inadequacy is of no importance. As long as she lives on love and raises her eyes to the eagle, he will carry her aloft on his wings and plunge her into the bosom of the Blessed Trinity, the eternal home of love. Thérèse expressed her relationship to Christ with this prayer: "I stay with my eyes fixed on you, longing to be the prey of your love. I hope that one day you will swoop upon me and carry me off to the furnace of love."[29] The metaphor of the dove here received its deepest significance.

Thinking Modeled on Scripture

Although Thérèse had some "peak experiences," a vision during a dream and some moments of ecstasy, these were exceptions rather than the rule. As we have seen before, her inner experiences were characterized by periods of spiritual darkness and uncertainty. She had met death, had gazed into the abyss of nothingness, and intelligent as she was, she recognized the arguments of the rationalists and agnostics of her time who rejected God and revelation. Thérèse lived in face of the existential question.

The value of Thérèse's testimony for our age is her option for faith and surrender to God in spite of the agnostic temptation. Her stand was based on insights that went beyond logic to an experience of the divine that consumed her. Radical as she was, she knew she had to give herself totally to Jesus and in doing so she found that Jesus responded with unmistakable directness. She knew Jesus had a special plan for her, that he guided her on a particular path and helped her to walk the way that suited her best.

What we can learn from Thérèse is the interaction between her self-understanding, based on her experience of life, and the inspired word of God. She allowed her thinking to be molded by that word. She saw her constructs refined and she acquired new ones so that, while remaining her own, they grew out to be a genuine Christian theology. She was right when she said, "One's most intimate thoughts, the children of one's heart and mind are riches which one clings to as one's very own."[30] It was these thoughts, remodeled by scripture, that made her the saint she was.

It is also good to notice Thérèse's use of metaphor in her self-understanding. This is not a sign of simplistic thinking. Thinking in images and metaphors is rather a very powerful means of understanding and expressing reality. Metaphor has always been the best tool of theology and worship, often much more expressive than abstract notions or theoretical definitions. When we call God "Father" or Jesus "the way," these metaphors carry a wealth of meaning that cannot be contained in speculative concepts. Perhaps we too could examine our own metaphors, the metaphors that best express our own position and task; perhaps we too could enrich our metaphors with the thoughts of scripture.

Thérèse's devotion to "the hidden face of Jesus" made her adopt a deliberate policy of covering her inner suffering with the veil of joy and contentment.[31] Thérèse lived her dramatic life, with its intense longing and fierce struggles, in a small convent, hidden from the world, hidden even from her own companions. She herself never suspected that her personal notes would make her inmost thoughts so public and widely known. It is, perhaps, one of these contradictions of which she herself was so conscious: the unusual in what is ordinary, greatness in smallness. Thérèse lived but a few years in very ordinary, humble circumstances, yet she had a genuine experience of God. It gives all of us, "little ones" like her, hope that we too may achieve some greatness in spite of our smallness.

Six
Francis of Assisi

If we were to take the stories about Francis at face value, he must have lived in a world constantly shot through with supernatural intrusions. When Francis preached, the birds of the air settled around him and fishes poked their heads out of the water to listen to him. When Francis prayed at night, angelic choirs could be heard providing appropriate background music. Francis frequently had visions. Christ appeared and spoke to him. He was shown scenes of things that were to happen in the future. In other words, Francis was a man who experienced God's presence in a very explicit and miraculous way.

A typical example of this might be what happened to Francis and his early companions while they were traveling in the valley of Spoleto. Having just founded his little band of mendicant friars, Francis could not make up his mind whether they should restrict themselves to prayer and contemplation or dedicate their lives to the active apostolate. It was, indeed, a very important decision. Should the future Franciscans spend their time praising God in total withdrawal from the world as true contemplatives? Or should they devote themselves to preaching and spiritual guidance in an effort to reform the church? In his *Life of St. Francis*, St. Bonaventure narrates that the brethren argued about it for a long time:

> But Francis, true servant of Christ, did not trust in his own efforts or those of his brethren. With urgent prayer he implored God to let him know His Divine will concerning the matter. Then he was illumined by a divinely

revealed oracle. He understood that he had been called by God to this purpose, that he might win back for Christ the souls that the Devil was trying to carry off. Therefore he decided to live rather for all men than for himself.[1]

What happened when Francis was "illumined by a divinely revealed oracle"? In the context of the other miracles and wonders, does it not suggest that Christ appeared to him in an aura of light and told him: "Francis, I want you to win back for me the souls the devil is trying to carry off"? Because we have never seen Christ appear to us in this fashion (nor, for that matter, enjoyed the sight of fishes poking their heads out of the water to listen to our words), we are inclined to switch off. And rightly so. For this type of thing does not happen to us. And, even if such things did really happen to St. Francis, it does not help us in the least. But by putting Francis' experiences on the shelf of medieval miracles, we may well be doing him, and ourselves, an injustice.

Revelations
There can be no doubt about it: The real events of Francis' life are encrusted with fanciful medieval elaboration. Yet, if we compare independent sources, we can reconstruct the historical events to a high degree of reliability. We have from the 13th century itself the *Little Flowers of St. Francis,* the two biographies by Thomas of Celano (1229 and 1247) and the *Life* written by St. Bonaventure (1263). We can add to this the *Mirror of Perfection,* which was compiled in 1318. As various traditions have been somewhat independently preserved in these books, we can detect accretions and uncover historical kernels by comparative study. This also helps us to understand how contemporaries of St. Francis interpreted his experience of the Divine.

Let us revert to the incident quoted above, to the

"divinely revealed oracle" that made Francis take up preaching. In the *Flowers of St. Francis* we read a slightly different version of what took place in those fateful days. Francis, we read, was in great uncertainty as to what God expected him to do with the newly founded order. Should the members be wholly intent on prayer or should they preach? "Greatly he desired to know the will of God concerning these things." The account then continues to narrate that Francis did not want to trust his own judgment or even his own prayers in the matter. So he decided to seek advice.

He called Friar Maffeo and sent him with the same request to Sister Clare and Friar Silvester. To both of them he sent this message: "Please, pray devoutly to God that He may be pleased to reveal to me which is the more excellent way: whether to give myself up to preaching or entirely to prayer." After some time Friar Maffeo returned from his mission, having separately taken advice from the two persons indicated. Both of them had come to the same conclusion. It is interesting to note how the reply was conveyed to St. Francis.

When Friar Maffeo returned, Francis treated him as a messenger from God. He washed his feet and set a meal before him. Then he took him aside for some distance into the forest, knelt down before him, bent his arms in the form of a cross, and asked of him, "What is it that my Lord Jesus Christ commands?" Friar Maffeo replied: "This is the answer that Friar Silvester and Sister Clare received from God: You should go forth to preach throughout the world. Christ has not chosen you for yourself alone, but for the salvation of others." When Francis had heard these words, he understood they expressed the will of Christ. He rose up and said with great fervor, "Let us then go forth in God's name."[2]

Here we have an interpretation of what St. Bonaventure meant with his "divinely revealed oracle." There was no apparition of Christ, no supernatural voice, not even an unusual ecstasy. Francis relied on the prayer and the insights of two holy persons. When their advice was communicated to him, in words similar to those spoken about Paul: "I have chosen him to serve me, to make my name known to Gentiles and kings" (Acts 9:15), Francis recognized in this a communication to him from Christ. The external guidance received and the testimony of his heart combined to reveal a manifestation of God's will.

With our 20th century everything-or-nothing approach, we might now draw the conclusion that nothing happened at all. Apparently we accept only full-scale miracles or the dull monotony of everyday life! Here is where we miss the point and where the Middle Ages can teach us something. Christ may not have appeared to Francis in his visible human form and radiant with light, but does this mean that Francis did not have a *real* experience of Christ in the event? Is it not likely that Francis, who was so open and sensitive to God's presence, perceived in a flash of insight that it was Christ himself who communicated his will in this way? Seen in this light, Bonaventure's statement is quite accurate: Francis *was* illumined by a divinely revealed oracle.

The Role of Scripture

Having gained this better understanding of St. Francis' spiritual experiences, we can examine with more confidence some other turning points in his life. If we do this, we will discover that Sacred Scripture played an important role in them.

What should St. Francis' followers be called? By what name should they become known? The *Mirror of Perfection* states that it was revealed to Blessed Francis that the order should be called the Order of Friars Minor. How was it revealed to him? From the available data, we can reconstruct the event as an insight resulting from prayerful reflection on the gospels. When Francis started his search for an appropriate name, he prayed about it. He wondered what name Christ himself would want to impose. He turned to the gospels for guidance. He was struck by two passages which were apparently unrelated: "There is no need to be afraid, little flock, for it has pleased your Father to give you the kingdom," and "Whenever you did this for one of the least important of these brothers of mine, you did it for me" (Lk 12:32,JB; Mt 25:40). Francis was struck by the fact that Christ addressed his apostles as "a *little* flock," that he used the term "the least of my brethren." It fitted exactly the image Francis had of what his followers should be; namely, small, little, the least, "minor." In this process of reflecting on these gospel texts and communicating with Christ about it, the words of the gospel were perceived by Francis as expressing a specific message of Christ to him. He experienced them as Christ talking to him directly. And so he could say in all truth: "Christ revealed to me that he wants us to be called the Order of the Friars Minor."[3]

A similar insight of St. Francis caused a new greeting to be used by his itinerant preachers. He told them to wish peace to everyone they met in words such as "May the Lord grant you peace!" or "Peace be to you!" Since people were not used to such a truly religious salutation, they used to laugh and make jokes about this singular custom. But Francis, who was extremely anxious to follow the Lord's injunctions to the letter, had grasped the importance of Christ's admonition to the apostles, "When you go into a house, say, 'Peace be with you' " (Mt 10:12). He could say, as he was to write in his testament, "The Lord revealed to me that I should say for a greeting: the Lord give you peace." This greeting marked him off as a spiritual messenger, as an apostle of Christ. So whenever a friar became discouraged by the ridicule of people, Francis could reply confidently: "Let them talk. These people do not perceive the things which are of God."[4] The remark was, indeed, to the point. What was lacking in them was spiritual perception.

Many of the "revelations" Francis received resulted from a prayerful listening to the word of scripture. Was it not the simple reading aloud of Mark 6:1-11 that set Francis off to a life of apostolic poverty? On that day early in his life when Francis was still groping for guidance regarding his way of life, he happened one day to attend Mass in a small church. The gospel that was read out contained Christ's admonition to his disciples that they should carry no money in their purses, no spare tunic. The text made an indelible impression on Francis. He was filled with unspeakable joy. He said, "This is what I desire, this is what I long for with all my heart!" Immediately after Mass, on leaving the church, he took off his shoes, laid aside his staff, his purse, threw away his mantle and walked away barefoot, possessing just one garment.[5] Later Francis was to say that this way of life had been communicated to him by a divine revelation.[6] Francis was aware of the fact that God speaks through scripture.

Being a Doer of the Word

Francis possessed an enormous faith in and respect for Sacred Scripture. Yet when we study his teaching, we do not find great stress on the reading of the inspired writings. He did not prescribe that every friar, or even every community of friars, should have its own copy of the Bible. Never, to my knowledge, did he enjoin the regular meditation of scripture or recommend that some members of the order be appointed for specialized studies in it. No, whenever the question of scripture studies came up, rather than favoring such external practices, Francis always reiterated the same message: Don't waste time in studying scripture. Rather, put in practice what it tells you to do. Be a doer of the Word and not just a hearer.

Francis was expressing by this a lesson he had experienced in his own life. The word of God only became real for him when he had put it into practice. His way of life consisted in nothing else but in taking Jesus' words literally. When he composed his first rule for the order, he did little more than string together quotations of gospel texts.[7] Even in its later formulation, the rule was for him no more than an effort to execute a program laid down in the gospels. Francis did not think of the gospel as a text in a book (as we unconsciously do), but as something affecting his life. And although he had scripture read out to him every day, he could easily dispense with it. On his deathbed he could say: "No, don't read Scripture to me now. There is no need of it. I carry the words of the Crucified One in my heart and in my bones."[8]

Once, when Francis was living at St. Mary of the Portiuncula, a poor woman came begging for food. It turned out that she was the mother of two of Francis' followers who lived in another community. Francis wanted to give her some money or something to eat, but the Minister General, Father Peter of Catana, told him: "We have nothing in the house that we could give her. The only thing of value we have is the copy of the New Testament from which we read the Lessons at Matins." As books had to be copied by hand in those days, such a volume was certainly a valuable possession. However, Peter would never have expected Francis' reaction when the latter told him: "Then give the copy to her. For it is much better to practice charity, as we are told to do by Scripture, than to keep reading Scripture and not practice it!"[9] It was doing the deed that mattered, not possessing the word.

Or consider the case of the novice who wanted to

possess a copy of the psalter. We may assume that the young man was filled with the best of intentions: He desired to pray the psalms more often and meditate on them in the course of the day. But Francis was reluctant to give him this permission, feeling that it would undermine the novice's vow of poverty. As they were sitting near the fire, Francis said: "After you have a psalter, you will desire to have a breviary. Then you will sit in your chair, like a great prelate, and say to your brother, bring me my breviary." Then Francis poured ashes on his head, put his hand on it and kept rubbing it around, saying, "I, a breviary! I, a breviary!" When the novice still did not get the point, Francis talked to him in this way: "My dear friend, in the past we had great heroes and warriors, such as Charlemagne, Roland and Oliver, and many other famous knights. They endured great trials and faced bitter hardship in fighting the Moors. Many died a martyr's death. Nowadays some bards go round who try to obtain honor, not by doing what these great men have done, but by singing about them. This may also be your temptation. Once you start reading books and talking about them, you will put your confidence in knowledge and not in virtuous deeds."[10]

Francis was to repeat this again and again. At times he said that learning would be the ruin of the order. "A time of hard testing will come. Then books will be useful for nothing. They shall be thrown in corners and cupboards." Francis' biographer adds that Francis was not opposed to the study of scripture itself, but to the tendency of people to think that learning could make up for practice.[11] St. Bonaventure records St. Francis' words on another occasion:

> "Yes, indeed, it is my will that priests who have been received in the order should devote themselves unto the study of Holy Scripture. But they should always remember to follow the example of Christ who, we read, prayed more than he studied. They may study as

long as they do not lose their zeal for prayer. Nor should they study only that they may know how they ought to speak. Rather they should study with this purpose in mind of becoming doers of the Word, and, after having done it, of setting forth to others what they should do."[12]

This is indeed plain language. It illustrates once more Francis' preoccupation with taking the word seriously.

Breaking Down Our Defenses

If we examine Francis' life in the way I have done above, he proves to be much closer to us than we might have originally thought. Francis' life was not different from ours in that it contained more miraculous happenings or divine manifestations. Francis was an ordinary person like ourselves, seeking God's will in a complicated world and a confused church. That Francis managed to make something of his life, he owed to his sensitivity; to being aware that God was speaking to him through the words of scripture; and to a determination to do the word rather than just hear it.

Could it be that we are too casual about reading the words of scripture or hearing them read out to us? Does the word of God fail to touch us because we lack Francis' sensitivity?

Psychology tells us that our subconscious is liable to build up defenses against things we are afraid of. One subtle defense mechanism against the effectiveness of scripture may be the illusion that what Christ says need not be taken literally. We keep telling ourselves that putting it into practice would be impractical, if not impossible. This was indeed the objection formulated by some cardinals at Pope Innocent III's court, when Francis tried to obtain approval for his rule. "Living in such a way," the cardinals maintained, "is a thing untried and too hard for human strength." We may perhaps be allowed to think that the cardinals, in voicing this objection, were subconsciously expressing their own reason for not observing the gospel more strictly. The bishop of Sabina deflated the objection by a simple observation: "This poor man is in fact asking us to approve the pattern of Gospel-life. Let us be careful not to make the Gospel of Christ a stumbling-block. For if anyone says that in the observance of Gospel perfection there is contained anything that is untried, or contrary to reason, or impossible to observe, he would clearly seem to contradict Christ himself, the author of the Gospel."[13]

If we sincerely seek to know God's will, he will reveal himself to us through the words of scripture as he did to Francis. If we are determined to be doers rather than just hearers, he will change our lives too.

Seven
Charles de Foucauld

On December 1, 1916, at Tamanrasset, deep in the
Moroccan Sahara, Bedouin soldiers entered the small
whitewashed house of the only European within hundreds of miles. He was the French missionary, Father
Charles de Foucauld. They ordered him to kneel
down. One pressed the barrel of his gun to the priest's
neck.

Charles was 58 years old. Born at Strasbourg,
brought up in a traditionally pious Catholic family,
he had lost his faith as a college student at Nancy. For
five years he had served as a French soldier in Algeria
and Morocco, a period of loose living and dissipation,
but also of adventure and courage. Then, after his conversion to Christ at the age of 28, his life had become totally geared to an ever increasing conformity
to his Master. He had spent seven years as a Trappist
contemplative, three as a solitary monk at Nazareth.
Ordained a priest in 1901, he had given 15 years of
Christian witness and priestly service in lonely out-
posts of the Tuareg mission. Now the moment to meet
his Master had come.

Charles' thoughts at that moment have not been
recorded. But we know from his letters and spiritual
notebooks that he had fully realized the risks inherent
in his undertaking. His mind was prepared for it. He
had lived in the shadow of death ever since he entered
Morocco as the first resident missionary.

> The less of everything we have, the more like the
> crucified Jesus we are. I should have nothing more or
> better than Jesus of Nazareth had it. . . . I should live
> today as though faced with the prospect of dying this

evening as a martyr. "One thing is necessary": to do at all times what would be most pleasing to Jesus, to be continually ready for martyrdom and accept it without a shadow of a defense, as did the divine Lamb, doing so in Jesus through Jesus and for Jesus."[1]

The soldier pulled the trigger. Charles was dead. But his influence did not die. His humility, his poverty of life, his apostolate through simple witness, have inspired new initiatives in the church. Many have decided to follow in his footsteps, chief among whom are the Little Brothers and Sisters of Charles de Foucauld. As the model of a new missionary approach, Charles continues to attract many to his lifestyle. Scores of books are written about this. What many people do not realize is that Charles' convictions came from daily meditations on the word of God, meditations which were for him a real experience of hearing God speak. It is this aspect of his life I will discuss in this chapter.

Hours With Jesus

When Charles decided not to take his final vows in the Trappist order, it was because even such a monastic life seemed to him too luxurious and protected. At his own request he lived in the Trappist monastery at Staoueli near Akbes in Syria. His cell was bare, his meals frugal. It was not poor enough for Charles. "To the rich we are poor, but we are not poor as our Lord was."[2] The monastic rules and regulations prevented the greater detachment, the more unconditional surrender he was dreaming of.

From 1897 to 1900 Charles realized his dream in Nazareth. He was employed as a servant of the Poor Clares. He slept in a little hut in the monastery garden, did manual work during the day and spent the rest of his time in study and meditation. It came as close to Jesus' hidden life as possible. In one of his meditations he has our Lord say:

"Look at the life I have fashioned for you: could it possibly parallel my hidden life more perfectly? . . . You are living it at Nazareth, unknown, inordinately poor, lonely in your smock and sandals, a poor servant to poor nuns. Some take you for a laborer of the lowest kind; others think you are an outcast; some think you are perhaps the son of a criminal. Most—nearly all, in fact—take you for a fool. You obey the nuns and the portresses as I obeyed my parents. You give orders to nobody, absolutely no one."[3]

Charles would get up at first light. On rising, he would say matins, then meditate on the gospels before going to the chapel to hear Mass. As he had the custom of jotting down what occurred to him during these gospel meditations, we have a fair idea of how he went about them and what form they took.

One of the methods used by Charles was the following: After reading the scripture text with great attention, he would first ask in prayer, "What do you want to say to me, O God?" Forcing himself to silence, and listening intently to God, he would, as it were, hear God put into words the message contained in the biblical text. He would write down these words as he knew God spoke them to him. Then he would make a declaration in response, "For my own part, this is what I want to tell you." After this, he would remain in God's presence in loving silence, "saying nothing else, gazing on the Beloved."[4] The message of the gospel meditation would remain with him throughout the day, especially during the periods he spent in adoration before the Blessed Sacrament.

In Luke 6:27-42, for example, Jesus tells us: "Love your enemies, do good to those who hate you, bless those who curse you. . . . If anyone hits you on one cheek, let him hit the other one too; . . . Give to everyone who asks you for something, and when someone takes what is yours, do not ask for it back. . . . Be merciful. . . . Do not judge others. . . . Why do you look at the speck in your brother's eye. . . ?" When meditating on this passage, Charles first prayed, "Speak to me, Lord, for your servant is listening!" Then Jesus' answer came to him:

> "All these commandments are the precepts of charity. You would not find them surprising if you could once and for all really grasp that all human beings together make up a single family. God is their common father, creator and preserver. He is father to all men equally. He loves all human beings incomparably more than the most loving father loves his children. . . . Carve deeply into the foundations of your soul the chief commandment from which all the others spring: all human beings are really and truly *brothers* in God. He is their common father. It is his will that all human beings should look on one another, love one another and treat one another in every way as the fondest of brothers."[5]

The part of scripture that inspired Charles most was the hidden life of Jesus. At the words, "They returned to their home town of Nazareth in Galilee" (Lk 2:39), Charles had an intimate conversation with Jesus through which he gave expression to his deepest convictions. The meditation can be reconstructed as the following dialogue:

> "After my presentation and my flight into Egypt, I withdrew to Nazareth. There I spent the years of my childhood and youth till I was thirty years of age. Once again, it was for your sake I went there, for love of you."

> "What was the meaning of that part of your life, Lord?"

> "I led it for your instruction. I instructed you continually for thirty years, not in words, but by my silence and example."

> "What was it you were teaching me, Lord?"

> "I was teaching you primarily that it is possible to do

good to men—great good, infinite good, divine good—without using words, without preaching, without fuss, but by silence and by giving them a good example."

"What kind of example, Lord?"

"The example of devotion, of duty towards God lovingly fulfilled, and goodness towards all men, loving kindness to those about one and domestic duties fulfilled in holiness. The example of poverty, lowliness, recollection, withdrawal, the obscurity of a life hidden in God, a life of prayer, penance, and withdrawal, completely lost in God, buried deep in him."[6]

Experience of God?

No one can fail to see that Charles' decisions and actions flowed from his interpretation of the gospels. Charles had internalized the gospel texts. Until his death he was to continue this practice of assimilating at a very deep level the example and words of his divine Master.

Did he have a tangible experience of God? There is no doubt he did. But, fortunately for us ordinary mortals, as far as we know, it never expressed itself in an extraordinary form. Charles did not claim to have visions, nor did he wake up at night to hear an audible voice. Charles had to meet God, as most of us have to, in the stillness of his heart.

Before his conversion Charles had prayed, "Oh God, if you exist, let me know of your existence." Charles' spiritual notes are a continuous testimony to the fact that God had heard this prayer. He had made himself known in an unmistakable manner. Never again would Charles doubt the presence of God, though at times God might hide his face. He could write: "I think I see my God clearly. Give me full enlightenment, oh God, so that I may act in the certain knowledge of doing your will, for this is the food by which I long to live always."[7] He also knew periods of darkness and confusion. "God sometimes allows us to be in such profound darkness that not a single star shines in our skies."[8] This is the ordinary experience of the believing Christian. He has heard God speak; he continues on his journey even in times of discouragement and desolation.

We can recognize the Spirit by the effects he produces: love, joy, peace, patience, kindness, goodness, faithfulness, humility and self-control (Gal 5:22-23). These were the signs by which Charles too knew that God was at work in him. The following excerpts speak for themselves:

> My spiritual life is filled with the presence of Our Lord.

> "You gave me a tender and increasing love for you, O Jesus, and a taste for prayer, trust in your word, a longing to imitate you."

> "You dwell in the faithful soul, my Lord: 'we shall come to it, and make our dwelling with it.' You become, as it were, the soul's soul; your grace supports it in all situations, enlightens its understanding, guides its will. It is no longer the soul that does things, but you in it. You give it life, the life of grace, the seed of the life in glory, in growing abundance. You give it truth, firmly establishing it, giving it a taste for it, opening its eyes to it, making it see things with the eyes of faith."

> "I am plunged deep in your mercies. I drown in them. They cover me, wrapping me round on every side."

> The state of my soul is unchanged: I am always full of joy, rejoicing at the feet of Jesus. The simplicity of my life is profoundly pleasant to me, these long lonely hours of prayer and reading, spent so simply. I am quite overcome, and I marvel at the way God guides my soul.[9]

Prayer and Action

We live in a time with heavy stress on Christian involvement. We are repeatedly warned of the danger of spiritual escapism. Christians have a task in the social and political liberation that is to be achieved within the present world; prayer and belief in afterlife cannot dispense a Christian from commitment to building up the kingdom of heaven on earth.

Involvement is, indeed, a Christian virtue, but isn't there a danger, too, of neglecting the spiritual dimension of life? Is our experience of God, perhaps, impoverished by an involvement that is too one-sidedly social and political?

Charles de Foucauld may teach us a lesson in this respect. Charles too believed in action. When he left Nazareth in order to be ordained a priest and when he decided to return to North Africa as a missionary, he did so because he was concerned about the people there. Charles was indignant about the injustices committed by the colonizing powers toward the indigenous population. Frequently he complained that the Europeans—government officials, soldiers, businessmen—had no real respect or regard for the original inhabitants of the country. They were only interested in furthering their own ends without real care for the others. Charles did not preach revolution nor did he mix in politics. Instead, he decided to give a counter-witness of love because he was convinced this is what Jesus would have done. He learned the Tuareg language. Both at Beni-Abbès and at Tamanrasset Charles lived among the ordinary people in a small house, sharing in their everyday joys and sorrows. As their "universal brother," he looked after the sick, cooking food for them and cleaning their wounds. When no rains fell for 17 months in 1907-1908, Charles helped as much as he could to fight general starvation. He distributed so much of his own stores to needy families that he himself fell ill with exhaustion and undernourishment. For long periods he traveled around as a nomad, living in a tent, constantly moving from place to place. Wherever he was, he tried to be friendly and accessible.

Charles realized that his own contribution could only be a small part in a much wider overall apostolate. He was convinced that the message of Christ would only penetrate the Muslim world if many more like himself were prepared to live a life of simple gospel witness among Muslims. That's why he worked hard at establishing a congregation of followers; why he insisted—with great farsightedness—that lay people would play a greater role in the mission of the future; why he dreamed of having a book published to appeal to idealistic Christian volunteers. Charles would, no doubt, have had great sympathy for nationalistic uprisings or the freedom struggles of oppressed social classes. But true to the gospel—and, perhaps, again with great farsightedness—he never put great hopes on changes effected by guns and bloodshed. For him, the kingdom of God could only come by a change of heart, by the testimony of the Spirit: love, concern, friendliness and charity.

Such a spiritual witness of love can be sustained only by a person who leads a spiritual life himself. Even in the midst of action and involvement, prayer should remain a constant source of strength and inspiration. It would be foolish to think that we can be really helpful to others if we lose contact with the wellspring from which our loving service should flow. Involvement can only be Christian when it is the expression of a loving experience of Christ working in us. This is, perhaps, an important lesson we can learn from Charles de Foucauld. Every Christian soldier is at heart a monk; in the middle of the battle there should be room for solitude.

Charles expresses this beautifully in a meditation on Jesus' public life:

"My God, here I am at your feet in my cell. It is night, everything is quiet, everything is sleeping. At this moment I am perhaps the only one in this town at your feet. What have I done to deserve such graces? Now I thank you, and how happy I am! I adore you from the depth of my heart, my God. I adore you with all my soul, and love you with all the strength that is in my heart. I am yours, yours alone. My whole being is yours. . . . Tell me, what was the manner of your public life, my Lord Jesus?"

[Jesus speaks:] "I strove to save men through speech and works of mercy, instead of being satisfied to save them by penance and prayer alone as I had been doing at Nazareth. My zeal for souls became externally apparent. Yet while my life became very public, it still preserved some of the qualities of the solitary life. I often withdrew for the night, or for several whole days in the solitude to prayer. It remained a life of prayer, penance and interior recollection. And apart from the time devoted to preaching the Gospel, it was a life of solitude."[10]

Prayer, says Charles, is sometimes accompanied by words—words of adoration; or love; or self-oblation, the giving to God of everything that one has. They can be words of thanksgiving for the goodness of God or for favors received. They may be words of apology in reparation for one's sins. They may be petitions for one's own needs or the needs of others. But prayer can also be without words. In fact, this may be the most perfect prayer if it is an expression of silent love. The greater our commitment to action, the more demanding our involvement in militant causes, the more we stand in need of creating space for such silent union with God.

Prayer is that state in which the soul looks wordlessly on God, solely occupied with contemplating him, telling him with looks that it loves him, while uttering no words, even in thought. . . . While everything is silent and asleep, while everything is drowned in darkness, I live at the feet of my God, pouring out my heart in love of him, telling him I love him, while he tells me I shall never love him as much as he loves me, however great my love may be. They are hours of incomparable happiness.[11]

Eight
Teresa of Avila

Sixteenth-century Spain was ruled by men. Men governed the homes and ran the family businesses. Men preached from the pulpits and lectured at universities. All positions of authority both in the church and in the state were held by men. "The very thought that I am a woman is enough to make my wings droop," Teresa used to say.[1] With good reason. When Teresa wrote a commentary on the Song of Songs, the manuscript was burned at the order of her confessor because he thought it "a dangerous innovation" that a woman should presume to touch on such a subject.[2] It is all the more remarkable then that Teresa managed to establish herself as a great church reformer and a theologian of lasting fame.

Teresa's career was like a storm that only gradually gathered momentum. Born at Avila in 1515, she entered a convent of Carmelite Sisters in 1536. For 17 long years she led the life of a "don't press me too hard," middle-of-the-road contemplative nun. In 1553 she experienced a second conversion, which was followed by nine years of an intense spiritual search. In the last 20 years of her life (1562-1582) she became a public figure, the recognized leader of the new Discalced Order of Carmelites, both for men and women. In this period she personally took part in the foundation of 18 new monasteries and convents, encouraging would-be candidates and instructing superiors, fighting off opponents, completing practical arrangements. She also proved a formidable writer. Apart from producing hundreds of meditations, letters, maxims and spiritual testimonies, she composed five major works: her autobiography, *Conceptions of the Love of God*, *The Way of Perfection*, the book of the *Foundations*, and *The Interior Castle*.

Teresa has the distinction of being the first of only two women who have been declared Doctor of the Church. She owed this recognition mainly to her teaching on prayer. Teresa always maintained that, given the right disposition, everyone could be led to higher states of prayer in which we come face to face with God in a tangible manner. In a short chapter like the present one, it is obviously not possible to cover all aspects of Teresa's teaching in this regard. It seemed to me that it would be more profitable, for our purpose, to restrict ourselves to some practical advice Teresa has to give on how to experience God through prayer, and that we might achieve this best by studying especially how one passage from the gospels, namely the one concerning the Samaritan woman, proved of great help to Teresa herself. We shall attempt to relive how God revealed himself to Teresa through this bible text in a very special manner.

In Her Father's Home

Don Alonso Sanchez de Cepeda and Donna Beatriz D'Avila Ahumada, Teresa's parents, possessed a small mansion in Santo Domengo Square in the center of Avila. It was a kind of compromise between a castle and a merchant's home popular with the lower nobility in those days. High, gray stone walls surrounded the property on all sides. Entering through the heavy oak door in the gateway facing the square, one came upon an inner court of cobblestone, with a fountain in the middle, colonnades on the sides and, in the corners, flights of stairs going up to living rooms on the first floor. The rooms upstairs were dark and somber, the furniture austere by our standards. In the course of the day, most activity would take place downstairs: in the colonnades, or in the kitchen rooms and parlors beyond the colonnades.

It was in this courtyard that Teresa spent a lot of time as a teenager, playing with her friends or talking to relatives who had come to visit. From eyewitness reports we may well imagine what she looked like: her long, black, wavy hair and her sparkling eyes; her orange skirt trimmed with black velvet galloons; the golden bracelet on her arm; the pendant on her satin blouse. Teresa was inquisitive and lively. We are told that, just like her mother, she had a taste for reading. Without the knowledge of the strict Don Alonso, mother and daughter devoured the romantic literature of the time, the many stories of gallant knights and their ladies.[3] Teresa joined in the adventurous games of her elder brothers. On one occasion she left Avila with Rodrigo "to go to the land of the Moors and die a martyr's death." At another time the two wrote a novel of their own, spinning a fantastic story of chivalry and heroism.

The Cepedas were deeply religious people. Statues and holy pictures could be seen in various rooms. One painting in particular was very dear to Teresa. It depicted the meeting of Jesus with the Samaritan woman, as narrated in John 4:4-42. Jesus was sitting by himself at the side of the well talking to the woman from Sychar who had come to draw water. Jesus was telling the woman that if she understood who he was, she would be the one asking for water: He could give her water that would slake her thirst forever. The painting bore the woman's response as an inscription: *"Domine, da mihi aquam,"* "Lord, give me that water." Teresa was intrigued by this episode in Jesus' life:

> Oh, how often I remember the living water of which the Lord spoke to the woman of Samaria! I am so fond of that Gospel. I have loved it ever since I was quite a

child—though I did not, of course, understand it properly then, as I do now—and I used often to beseech the Lord to give me that water.[4]

Teresa had often read this gospel passage. Explanations had been given her in sermons and instructions. She must have gazed upon the painting many times, as children do with objects they like, and in her youthful fantasy she must have seen herself standing there in front of Jesus! It spoke to her imagination, this being alone with Jesus and speaking to him face to face. It helped her to pray. It made her ask for that mysterious water that wells up within the soul unto eternal life, and which Jesus alone can give.

In the Convent of the Incarnation

When Teresa became a nun, she brought with her a set of contradictory motives. On the one hand, the religious atmosphere at home, periods of reflection during illness, a previous stay in a convent and the reading of the lives of saints had engendered in her a genuine desire to dedicate herself to religion. On the other hand, her natural talents and interests, her pleasure in companionships and her popularity with friends and acquaintances, drew her to social involvement. As the rules of the convent were rather lax, she spent a good deal of time entertaining guests, visiting the homes of friends (sometimes for weeks on end) and taking part in the affairs of society.

When, through a combination of factors, it dawned on Teresa in 1553 that she was living the life of a halfhearted religious and that God called her to a higher commitment, the episode of the Samaritan woman began to play a new role in her life. She began to understand that she would never be able to raise herself from her lukewarmness, that Jesus would have to give her that living water of grace that alone could make her into a truly spiritual person. When Teresa's father died in 1543, Teresa asked for the painting of the Samaritan woman as a part of her inheritance, and she hung it in her cell as a treasured possession. Now Teresa would spend long periods kneeling in front of the painting and repeating with all her heart that ardent petition: "Lord, give me that water."

> "O life, who gives life to all! Do not deny me this sweetest water that you promise to those who want it. I want it, Lord, and I beg for it, and I come to you. Don't hide yourself, Lord, from me, since you know my need and that this water is the true medicine for a soul wounded with love of you."[5]

It was in this period that an incident happened that showed how much the painting meant to Teresa. She had read in a book that it was an imperfection for religious persons to possess ornate paintings. As Teresa had just made up her mind to live according to the strict observance of apostolic poverty, she was troubled in conscience about the painting of Jesus and the Samaritan woman she had in her cell. It was the only costly object she still had; others had been given away in an earlier purge. Teresa felt upset and confused. She argued to herself that anything more than paper images conflicted with religious poverty. But then, had this religious painting not helped her in her devotion to Christ? With her characteristic common sense and sound judgment, she eventually decided to retain the painting. Her love for Christ was more important than poverty or mortification. "Since love is better than poverty, I should not renounce everything that awakens my love."[6] She gave away the heavy frame with its "many carvings and adornments," but kept the picture itself.

Like many of her contemporaries, Teresa made good use of religious images. She complained of a poor imagination, of not having the ability as others had of representing persons or things in one's mind. She found this particularly frustrating when she tried to think of Christ. She states: "I have never succeeded to picture him within myself no matter how much I read about his beauty or how many images I have seen of him. I am then like a person who is blind or in darkness."[7] She says this was one reason why she liked images so much: They helped her to focus attention on Christ. The painting of Christ and the Samaritan woman was of special value to her because it fulfilled precisely this function. "I always carried with me a painting of this episode of the Lord at the well, with the words inscribed: 'Lord, give me water.' "[8]

The Water of Life

It was after 1553 that Teresa began to have what she called her "supernatural" experiences. Certain things began to happen to her while she was at prayer and she knew they were brought about by God. Yet the developments were so startling and unexpected that in the beginning she did not know how to respond to them. On no account did she want to become a prey to illusions and hallucinations. By vigorous self-examination, by discussion with saintly men and theologians and, most of all, by continued searching in prayer, she gained an understanding of how God was drawing her to himself. Being so deeply involved herself and having analyzed the process as carefully as she did, she acquired unique insights into how we get close to God. Few theologians have taught as eloquently and clearly as she did how we can experience God.

In a nutshell, Teresa's doctrine can be summarized as follows: If we want God to take hold of us, we have to make time for "mental prayer." This means that apart from whatever vocal prayers we may be accustomed to saying, we need to set time aside for meditating about God and for speaking to him in our own words. Mental prayer basically consists in talking to God as we would to a very close and dear friend.

Mental prayer is a seeking of contact with God, a desire to get to know and love him better, time spent in his company.

Such mental prayer requires an effort on our part. God usually expects us to take some trouble before he shows his hand. In the beginning, mental prayer will consist in our reading some scripture passage, our thinking about the implications, our formulating some prayer in response and making various acts of the will, such as expressions of repentance, resolve, love and desire. But at a certain stage God takes over. At first in very small ways, then in a very noticeable manner God makes his presence felt, so that gradually we find that prayer is not something we are doing, but something God is working in us. These actions of God in our soul are "supernatural" experiences that help us greatly in committing ourselves more fully to God.

Teresa teaches that such experiences are open to all. She describes how God makes himself known to us in the initial stages. It may be that all of a sudden we know, not just notionally, but as an indisputable fact, that God is present with us. We feel his loving gaze on us, we sense his nearness in an indescribable manner. Then again, something may happen in us which Teresa calls "recollection." It is as if we withdraw into our inmost self, as if deep within us our will is clasped by a mysterious force. At other times we may unexpectedly feel our soul flooded with a sense of peace and joy. In this "prayer of quiet" we experience a great happiness and tranquillity different from anything we ever experienced before.

If we respond to these initial manifestations of God, he may well lead us on to higher forms of mystical awareness. Among these, Teresa mentions ecstasy or rapture; feeling God's touch by a "spiritual wound"; being so close to God that we see him, as it were, before us or hear him speak; enjoying mystical union. These peak experiences too are open to all, but, Teresa says, few people walk the narrow road that leads to them.

To explain the different stages we can go through, Teresa compares mental prayer to watering a garden. She says there are four ways of doing this: We may draw water from a well, which is laborious and produces little effect; we may turn the water wheel (this too involves a lot of work, but produces better results); we may have an irrigation system (which requires even less effort on our part); or we may receive a plentiful rain (in which case we need not do anything at all). So too, in prayer we often have to exert a lot of effort without feeling much profit. We are, as it were, laboriously drawing water from the well of our own thinking. Everything changes when God starts giving us the living water of spiritual experiences that well up in our hearts by themselves. "Love is continually bubbling up in them. . . It reminds me of little springs which I have seen gushing up and which keep on incessantly stirring up the sand all around them."[9] Teresa saw that this was the living water about which Christ had spoken to the woman of Samaria.

Many people, Teresa says, are very close to receiving a direct experience of God. But because they have not had the taste for it, they neglect the practice of mental prayer and allow themselves to be distracted by other things. The gospel text of the Samaritan woman received a totally new message for her in this light. Jesus told the Samaritan woman:

"If you only knew what God is offering
and who it is that is saying to you:
Give me a drink,
you would have been the one to ask,
and he would have given you living water. . . .

"Anyone who drinks the water that I shall give
will never be thirsty again;
the water that I shall give

will turn into a spring inside him, welling up to eternal life" (Jn 4:10-14,JB).

If people would only understand what Jesus is promising here, if only they were to taste the water he is offering to them, they would do everything in the world to obtain this water.

> I am very sorry for them. They seem to me like people who are very thirsty and see water a long way off. . . . their strength has come to an end; their courage has failed them. . . though perhaps they are only a couple of steps from the fountain of living water, of which the Lord said to the Samaritan woman that whoever drinks of it shall not thirst again. How right and how very true is that which comes from the lips of truth himself! In this life the soul will never thirst for anything more, although its thirst for things in the life to come will exceed any natural thirst that we can imagine here below. How the soul thirsts to experience this thirst![10]

There is nothing we can do to force Christ to give us the living water of a supernatural experience. But if we remain faithful to the practice of mental prayer, if we humbly and patiently wait for him to show his hand, if we earnestly seek him and keep asking, "Lord, give me that water," we can be sure that Christ will fulfill our request.

> "If any man is thirsty, let him come to me!
> Let the man come and drink who believes in me!"
> As scripture says: From his breast shall flow fountains of living water (Jn 7:37-38,JB).

> Remember, the Lord invites us all; and, since he is truth itself, we cannot doubt him. If his invitation were not a general one, he would not have said: "I will give you to drink." He might have said: "Come, all of you, for after all you will lose nothing by coming; and I will give drink to those whom I think fit for it." But, as he said we were all to come, without making this condition, I feel sure that none will fail to receive this living water unless they cannot keep to the path.[11]

Teresa of Avila

Laboring for Christ

Teresa's mystical experiences did not stop her from bearing many harassing responsibilities. To get an idea of what this meant, let us consider Teresa's position at Avila in 1572. In the preceding years she had been exceedingly occupied in establishing new foundations of her Discalced Order. In just three years' time (1568-1570) she had assisted in setting up five new convents and two monasteries. In 1571 she founded the convent at Alba de Tormes and then became temporary prioress of the convent at Medina del Campo, an earlier foundation, to consolidate the community. Then, quite unexpectedly, she was commanded by the apostolic delegate to become prioress of the Convent of the Incarnation at Avila, the convent where she had originally joined but which had refused to join the reform.

Teresa balked at the appointment. She knew the situation at the Incarnation only too well. Most of the 130 nuns in this convent would object to a tightening of the rule as the apostolic delegate demanded: They were used to their frequent visits to relatives' houses, to wearing jewelry over their habits, to organizing parties with music and dancing and to endless gossiping in one another's cells. Moreover, even the well-intentioned nuns in the community resented the fact that Teresa had been imposed from above, not elected according to custom. Teresa once wrote, "I fear a discontented nun more than I fear many devils." In the Convent of the Incarnation she would have to face 130 discontented nuns! This was something she had not bargained for. Starting a new foundation with a group of novices keen on living a life of perfection was one thing; being forced to discipline a battalion of unwilling nuns was quite another!

At first Teresa was firmly resolved not to accept the assignment. Then, while at prayer, it came to her mind that she should be ready to do anything for even the least of Christ's brethren. She heard Christ complain to her: "Those nuns in the Incarnation are sisters of mine and you hold back from helping them!"[12] Full of misgivings, she decided to go. On October 6, 1571, she came to the convent to be installed by the Carmelite Provincial. The reception was a disaster. A large body of nuns refused her entrance. When some supporters tried to clear a way for her, a man-to-man fight broke out. The local police had to be called. Only under armed protection could Teresa be taken to the chapel and officially inducted as the prioress.

The ensuing months in the winter of 1571-1572 tried Teresa's organizational and diplomatic skills to the extreme. Not only did she have to win the goodwill of the inmates of the convent in spite of having to introduce unpopular restrictions, she also had to solve practical problems such as where to find food for the sisters and how to make the community self-supporting. An exaggerated dependence on relatives and benefactors was one of the causes leading to the decline of the religious spirit. So Teresa cajoled, argued, encouraged, instructed, wrote letters and worked at the spinning wheel from morning till night. But all her many worries and activities did not lessen her union with God through prayer. A person who truly loves God, she says in her *Conceptions of the Love of God* written in those months, "delights in imitating, in some degree, the most toilsome life led by Christ."[13]

Again, it was the gospel text of the Samaritan woman that had a special message for her in those days. As soon as the woman from Sychar understood that Jesus was a prophet, she ran back to her village to brings others to him.

> I have just remembered some thoughts which I have often had about that holy woman of Samaria, who must have been affected this way. So well had she understood the words of the Lord in her heart that she left

the Lord himself so that she might profit and benefit the people of the village. This is an excellent example of what I am saying. As a reward for this great charity of hers, she earned the credence of her neighbors and was able to witness the great good which our Lord did in that village. . . . This woman, in her divine inebriation, went crying aloud through the streets. To me the astonishing thing is that they should have believed a woman—and she cannot have been a woman of much consequence, as she was going to fetch water. Great humility she certainly had; for, when the Lord told her of her sins, she was not annoyed (as people are nowadays—they find it difficult to stand home truths) but told him that he must be a prophet. In the end, her word was believed; and merely on account of what she had said, great crowds flocked from the city to the Lord. . . . This, I think, must be one of the greatest comforts of all—I mean to see good coming to souls through one's own agency.[14]

The Power of a Scripture Text

Throughout this short sketch I have been adducing examples of how the passage of the Samaritan woman played a role in various stages of Teresa's religious life. Was this the only passage that inspired Teresa? Obviously not. Other scripture texts too made a lasting impression on her, such as the conversion of Mary Magdalene (Lk 7:36-50),[15] or such phrases as, "My delight is to be with the children of men" (Prv 8:31).[16] But it remains true that the gospel text of the Samaritan woman fascinated her in a special way. It is worth investigating its implications.

Sacred Scripture was for Teresa the universal norm of faith and the most important source book for her meditations. In this sense she frequently stressed the validity of the whole Bible. No experiences, however supernatural they may seem, no teachings, however plausible they might be, can be from God if they are not in conformity with scripture.[17] Teresa was resolved to carry out with all her might even the smallest command contained in scripture.[18] For inspiration and guidance she turned in preference to scripture, especially the gospels. "I have always been fond of the words of the Gospels and have found more recollection in them than in the most carefully planned books."[19] Yet she also saw that some passages of scripture have a relevance for certain individuals that they don't have for others. In a very revealing discussion on the Canticle of Canticles, she expressed her exasperation with those who either laugh at the allusions of love between the bride and bridegroom or feel embarrassed by them. For some people, she wrote, these same verses had been extremely helpful. "I know someone who for many years had misgivings about this and nothing could reassure her until it pleased the Lord that she should hear some texts from the Canticles from which she realized that her soul was being well guided."[20] Although the scripture has a universal validity, not all parts are equally relevant to every individual. To a particular person God may speak more through one text than through many other ones.

This is an important realization in our attitude toward scripture. Although there is an objective meaning in the Bible valid for all, there is also a specific message different for each person. In some way this is true in every form of communication in which the same message is addressed to a multiplicity of persons. According to the principle, "The message is in the hearer," each person receiving the message will interpret it in his or her own way. This is all the more true in the case of scripture when God uses it to establish a link with a particular man or woman. Certain texts then assume a highly personal and specific relevance, eminently meaningful in the circumstances and expectations of the person concerned.

John 4:4-42 was such a text for Teresa. We have seen how profoundly it influenced her and how it repeatedly acquired new relevance in successive situations. As a young girl Teresa was intrigued by the face to face encounter with Christ; then by the woman's pleading for help. Later Jesus' words on the "living water" became a great source of enlightenment and encouragement regarding her experiences of the Divine. Then again, the Samaritan woman's return to Sychar strengthened Teresa in her own resolve to bring others to Christ. To Teresa it must have looked as if the story of the Samaritan woman had been specially inspired for her, that it had been given as a model to express different realities of her life: her previous sins and lukewarmness, her encounter with Christ, her taste of the living water, her apostolate of love. Throughout her life Christ spoke to Teresa in the words of John 4:4-42; she always discovered new meaning and confirmation in these words; they became a pattern of her vocation.

We would do well to recognize that each one of us has favorite texts, meaningful to us in a way they can never be to others. We are not mistaken in thinking that such passages may well have been specially inspired for us. Or, at least, we are correct in considering that the special relevance these verses have for us are a genuine part of God's inspired intention. For scripture is meant to address us also as individuals, to touch our hearts and our lives where they are different from others. We would do well, like Teresa, to treasure such choice texts, to integrate them ever more fully into our lives. After all, it isn't the multiplicity of scripture passages, but the depth to which some passages penetrate, that will determine the efficacy of God's word in our life.

It is also useful to reflect on the visual representation with which Teresa intensified her self-identification with the Samaritan woman. We have already mentioned how she refused to give up the painting of the incident at the well when she was undergoing her second conversion. Then she decided to keep it with her because it strengthened her love for Christ. Also, later on, she kept feeling the need of having some representation of the event with her in her first new foundation, the Convent of St. Joseph (1562), so she constructed a well in the middle of the compound which she called "The Fountain of the Samaritan woman." She also commissioned an artist to make a painting depicting the scene. Presumably she had left the other painting in the Convent of the Incarnation. In Medina del Campo (1567) there was a little hut in the garden which she called the resting place of the Samaritan woman. Time and time again we meet this need of keeping the encounter between Jesus and the Samaritan woman alive through concrete things and visible images. In this respect Teresa was a child of her times. Statues, paintings and buildings were still used as visible extensions of scripture. But Teresa's action also demonstrates a general human need. By following her example we may enrich our own experience of the scriptural text.

Teresa was a balanced person. She liked to be left alone in prayer and reflection, yet never shunned hard work or heavy responsibilities. She could talk about sublime things in straightforward and down-to-earth language. At times she could be lost in speechless ecstasy for hours; at other times she was humble enough to seek comfort in the simple words of scripture, especially those of her favorite texts. She enjoyed the highest forms of contemplation, but was never ashamed to admit that visual representations helped her. Perhaps it needed the mind and heart of a woman to experience and express the "wholeness" of a life of prayer.

Nine
Simone Weil

"As I worked in the factory, the affliction of others entered into my flesh and my soul. . . . There I received forever the mark of a slave, like the branding of the red-hot iron which the Romans put on the forehead of their most despised slaves. Since then I have always regarded myself as a slave."[1] These were the words of Simone Weil, teacher by profession, philosopher and mystic by nature, champion of intellectual liberty. She was appalled by the violence in modern society, the oppression of the weak, the fatigue and humiliation of industrial work.

Born in a middle-class Jewish family at Paris in 1909, she obtained her teacher's training certificate in 1931. She left France with her parents for the United States in 1942—to evade capture by the Germans. After six months she returned to England to offer her services to the Free French. She died there of consumption in August of 1943. The 12 years of her adult life can be described as a series of adventures and involvements. As a teacher at La Puy she helped industrial workers obtain a pay raise by pleading their cause in the press and joining them in public demonstrations and protest marches. In 1934 she quit school and took employment as a laborer, first in the Alsthom Metal Works, then in the Ateliers de Basse-Indre at Boulogne, and finally in the Renault factory outside Paris. She took up teaching again, and then, in 1936, she went to Barcelona to offer her services as a volunteer in the Spanish war, an episode that ended after a few weeks when she had to be evacuated on account of an accident in which she scalded her hand with oil. Between further teaching assignments she worked in the vineyards of Saint-Marcel-d'Ardèche. Although her health was rarely good she kept going back to physical work.[2]

Simone Weil is not remembered first and foremost as a social activist. During her life she had few friends, and she never attracted much public attention. At her funeral only seven people were present. It was her thoughts and ideas that captured the imagination of many when her not too voluminous letters and essays were published posthumously. This was actually exactly what she had hoped for. She cherished her thoughts and hoped that some day they might benefit other people, though she could not see how this might happen. In one of her last letters she says: "It is a great sorrow for me to fear that the thoughts which have come down into me should be condemned to death."[3] Knowing that many people today read her notes and are inspired by them would have been a great consolation to her.

For Simone the most fundamental laws of life are to love and to adhere to truth. These two laws are an inalienable part of our human make-up, they are the warp and woof of our existence. No collective authority, church or state or whatever, can in any way diminish these individual rights or limit them as obligations. Our love by its very nature has to stretch as widely as the whole of space, and our intelligence should reach out to all reality without any restriction or prejudice. Our minds should operate with unlimited freedom and complete impartiality.[4]

In this, Simone is a true prophet of our times. Perhaps never before in human history has the need for intellectual honesty, sincerity in behavior and frankness of speech been universally acclaimed as in our own days. Christ said, "The truth will set you free" (Jn 8:32) but truth has usually come out second best in the age-old struggle with diplomacy, cowardice and ambition. The emergence of the scientific method and the philosophy of the Enlightenment prepared the way for an enormous re-evaluation of sincerity and truth in our own days. Simone felt this need in the marrow of her bones.

The first duty resulting from our surrender to truth is to be absolutely natural and objective, to guard ourselves against preconceived ideas. The mind should be receptive to whatever information is offered to it and should judge by the available evidence. Tilting the balance this way or that to suit one's own party or to support a favorite theory is a serious denial of the highest vocation. "The degree of intellectual honesty which is obligatory for me, by reason of my particular vocation, demands that my thought should be indifferent to all ideas without exception, including for instance materialism and atheism."[5] The mind should be like water which allows all kinds of objects to fall into it; whether they float or sink to the bottom is not due to the water but to the weight of the objects themselves.

To allow the mind to exercise this function, it should be accorded perfect freedom. For the common good, people may be protected against theories that have not been proved or propaganda that causes social unrest. But on no account may the individual himself be punished or may his thinking be stifled. "The special function of the intelligence requires total liberty, implying the right to deny everything, and allowing no domination."[6] This, Simone maintained, applies equally to the church. A dissenting Christian may, in certain circumstances, be forbidden to spread his doctrines; never should he on that account be put under a penalty or excluded from the sacraments. The right to have one's own thoughts, even if they are mistaken, cannot be expropriated by the church.

Simone was a radical freethinker. And she remained a freethinker even after accepting Christ. She criticized the church for not being objective in its appraisal of spiritual values in other religions (thus anticipating statements of the Second Vatican Council) and pointed out the precarious condition of the theologian, who has both to defend pre-defined doctrine and be true to his own intellectual convictions. "Almost since the beginning, the individual has been ill at ease in christianity, and this uneasiness has been notably one of the intelligence. This cannot be denied."[7] Yes, she was a critic and a humanist, but one with a difference: She believed in God and in salvation through Jesus Christ. "Humanism was not wrong in thinking that truth, beauty, equality are of infinite worth, but in thinking that man can obtain them for himself without grace."[8]

Pagan Christian

In many ways Simone is an extraordinary and controversial figure.[9] The ancient rule that saints should be admired, not imitated, may well apply to her. That is, if we may consider her a saint of some kind or other. Because certain decisions she took may seem so strange and paradoxical that they call for a special kind of understanding. But, then, has the church not known such extraordinary figures as St. Simon, who spent years of his life sitting on a pillar, or St. Benedict Labre, who never took a bath?

What upsets most law-abiding Christians about Simone is her steadfast refusal to be baptized. Simone was convinced that Christianity was a revealed religion. She believed in Jesus Christ and accepted Catholic doctrine as true. She loved Catholic liturgy, hymns, architecture, rites and ceremonies. After her conversion she used to attend Mass regularly and spend hours in adoration of the Blessed Sacrament. In spite of all this, she did not want to enter the church and so join the Mystical Body of Christ.

She has explained her position in a number of letters. One of her reasons was that she had great difficulty in accepting the church as an institution. She knew that Christ had instituted a body of his followers and realized that some kind of social organization was unavoidable. Yet she could not forget the many injustices that had flowed from the church as a collective body in preceding centuries: the political wars fought in the name of religion, the persecution of heretics, the oppression of social classes. Coming in as an outsider she was also painfully aware of the many human aspects inherent in the present church structure. "I am kept outside the Church. . . not by the mysteries themselves but the specifications with which the Church has thought good to surround them in the course of centuries."[10] "Apart from pure mysticism, Roman idolatry has defiled everything."[11] "I have not the slightest love for the Church in the strict sense of the word. . . . I am capable of sympathizing with those who have this love, but I do not feel it."[12]

She also had a more positive reason for hesitating to be baptized. She felt closely affiliated in thought and affection to large groups of humanity and to many human values which, she feared, were kept outside the realm of the church.

> So many things are outside the Church, so many things that I love and do not want to give up, so many things that God loves, otherwise they would not be in existence. All the immense stretches of past centuries except the last twenty are among them; all the countries inhabited by colored races; all secular life in the white peoples' countries; in the history of these countries, all the traditions banned as heretical, those of the Manicheans, and Albigenses for instance; all those things resulting from the Renaissance, too often degraded but not quite without value.[13]

She argued that all such realities should be Catholic by right, but are excluded in present-day practice. She was convinced that God wanted her to express this Catholicity by refusing to be separated from them through baptism.

> You can take my word for it too that Greece, Egypt, ancient India and ancient China, the beauty of the world, the pure and authentic reflections of this beauty in art and science, what I have seen of the inner recesses of human hearts where religious belief is unknown, all these things have done as much as the visible christian ones to deliver me into Christ's hands as his captive. I think I might even say more. The love of those things which are outside visible christianity keeps me outside the Church.[14]

Such a stand may initially seem unintelligible. But on second thought it is strangely moving and has a compelling prophetic value. It reminds us that our solidarity with all men and women and the universality of God's presence in all religious search precede our Christian faith. Simone may not have been right in denying herself baptism; she was right in pointing out the danger of cutting ourselves off from our most basic solidarity through a partisan understanding of the church. Though outside the church, Simone said, she hoped she was inside the church in a different sense, or rather that she was on the threshold. She was convinced that this was where God wanted her to remain, loyal to Christ but also loyal to his presence in people outside Christianity.

Captive of Christ

It was this unusual woman who had a very direct experience of Christ. To appreciate what happened to her we should know that from her youth she had been educated an agnostic and that explicit religion had played little part in her life. Her home had been atheistic; her education totally indifferent to Christianity.

As soon as I reached adolescence I saw the problem of

God as a problem of which the data could not be obtained here below, and I decided that the only way of being sure not to reach a wrong solution, which seemed to me the greatest possible evil, was to leave it alone. So I left it alone.

The very name of God had no part in my thoughts.

In those days I had not read the Gospel.

I had never read any mystical works because I had never felt any call to read them.

I had never prayed. I was afraid of the power of suggestion that is in prayer.

Until last September (1941) I had never once prayed in all my life, at least not in the literal sense of the word. I had never said any words to God, either out loud or mentally.[15]

On two previous occasions Christianity had made an impression on her. The first time was the summer of 1935 while she was with her parents on holiday in a small fishing town in Portugal. On the feast of the local patron saint she watched the women march in procession round the ship, singing very ancient hymns "of a heart-rending sadness." It came to her in a flash of insight that Christianity was the religion of slaves and that she should really belong to it, as she was a slave herself. The second occasion was a visit to Assisi, two years later, when she was overwhelmed by a profound religious feeling in the chapel of St. Mary of the Angels. These contacts predisposed her, in a general sense, but they did not make her pray or read the gospel or other spiritual literature.

The meeting with Christ came in the monastery of Solesmes in 1938 during Holy Week. Solesmes was famous for its Gregorian chant and perfect Roman liturgy. In spite of the splitting headaches she was suffering from in those days, a residue of neglected sinusitis, she enjoyed the beauty of the music and the meaning of the words. "In the course of these services the thought of the passion of Christ entered into my being once and for all."[16] She was also helped by a young English Catholic who was a visitor at the monastery and who talked to her occasionally. She was struck by the angelic radiance on his face after he had received Communion. In one of their conversations her new friend talked about English poets of the 17th century who had written mystical works and recommended them to her. Simone took the trouble to read them and was immediately intrigued.

A Poem on Christ

There was in particular one poem, entitled "Love," by George Herbert (1592-1633), which took her fancy. She liked it very much. She learned it by heart. She used to repeat it often, as she says, "concentrating all my attention upon it and clinging with all my soul to the tenderness it enshrines."

The poem is, indeed, a gem of spiritual insight. Christ, love personified, invites us to enter his home. When, conscious of our sinfulness we hesitate to come forward, Christ overrules all our objections and makes us sit at his table. We need not be afraid of him. He knows our human nature because he created it; he has forgiven our sins because he died for them. The poem expresses the essence of the gospel message.

> Love bade me welcome; yet my soul drew back,
>> Guiltie of dust and sinne.
> But quick-ey'd Love, observing me grow slack
>> From my first entrance in,
> Drew near to me, sweetly questioning
>> If I lack'd any thing.
> "A guest," I answer'd, "worthy to be here:"
>> Love said, "You shall be he."
> "I the unkinde, ungratefull? Ah my deare,
>> I cannot look on thee."
> Love took my hand, and smiling did reply,
>> "Who made the eyes but I?"

"Truth Lord, But I have marr'd them: let my shame
            Go where it doth deserve."
"And know you not, sayes Love, who bore the
    blame?"
            "My deare, then I will serve."
"You must sit down," sayes Love, "and taste my
    meat:"
            So I did sit and eat.[17]

During one of the times that Simone recited this poem she had a direct experience of Christ. Without her realizing it, as she confessed later on, the recitation must have assumed the virtue of a prayer. Then, unexpectedly, "Christ himself came down and took possession of me. . . . In this sudden possession of me by Christ, neither my senses nor my imagination had any part; I only felt in the midst of my suffering the presence of a love, like that which one can read in the smile on a beloved face."[18] The experience took her totally by surprise. It had never occurred to her that this might happen.

> In my arguments about the insolubility of the problem of God I had never foreseen the possibility of that, of a real contact, person to person, here below, between a human being and God. I had vaguely heard tell of things of this kind, but I had never believed in them. . . . God in his mercy had prevented me from reading the mystics, so that it should be evident to me that I had not invented this absolutely unexpected contact.[19]

It was this experience that made her study the gospel. She reread the Greek classics and discovered they were "bathed in christian light." She noticed how the Bhagavad-Gita is filled with "words of such a christian sound." And, most of all, she learned the Our Father in the original Greek and made it her life prayer. "I had made a practice of saying it through once each morning with absolute attention."

The Our Father became for her the vehicle of a

regular mystical experience. "Although I experience it each day, it exceeds my expectation at each repetition." The prayer usually brought her into a state of metaphysical ecstasy.

> At times the very first words tear my thoughts from my body and transport it to a place outside space where there is neither perspective nor point of view. The infinity of the ordinary expanses of perception is replaced by an infinity to the second or sometimes the third degree. At the same time, filling every part of this infinity of infinity, there is silence, a silence which is not an absence of sound but which is the object of a positive sensation, more positive than that of sound. Noises, if there are any, only reach me after crossing this silence.[20]

This experience of limitless reality was sometimes enlarged by a distinctly different sensation, namely, the presence of Christ.

> Sometimes, also, during this recitation or at other moments, Christ is present with me in person, but his presence is infinitely more real, more moving, more clear than on that first occasion when he took possession of me.[21]

We may well ask ourselves, what was it that predisposed Simone to receive such exceptional graces? Why was she gifted with experiences denied to many a baptized Christian?

Attention

Simone had developed a remarkable intellectual and moral attitude which she had labeled "attention." She tells us more or less how she made the discovery. As an adolescent of 14, she went through a stage of great despondency. Through her studies and contacts she had come to see that some people in this world attain a degree of true greatness while others do not. By sheer intellectual brilliance and integrity of character some men and women rise above the ordinary level of existence. They are the geniuses who understand things others don't and who are in contact with truth. A deep fear had gripped Simone that this realm would be outside her reach.

She tells us that this realization had come upon her mainly because her brother André, older than herself by three years, seemed to overshadow her. He was excellent in his studies, possessed an exceptional memory and could make penetrating remarks. Simone felt that she herself was much inferior in comparison. She feared she might be condemned to remain forever on the level of what is second rate, superficial and trite. She was so dejected at this that, she says, even the thought of dying came to her mind.

It was in this period that she discovered the meaning of "attention." It came to her as a profound and liberating insight. The mark of true genius is not natural intelligence, but what we do with our intelligence. We do not reach the realm of truth unless we consciously raise our minds above what is superficial and deceptive. It is not natural disposition that lifts us to a higher plane of awareness, but a sincere effort to be open and to learn. It is concentrated attention that leads us to truth and brings us to fulfillment.

> I suddenly had the everlasting conviction that any human being, even though practically devoid of natural faculties, can penetrate to the kingdom of truth reserved for genius, if only he longs for truth and perpetually concentrates all his attention upon its attainment.[22]

After this event, attention dominated Simone's conduct and thought. With her strong will she internalized it to such a degree that it has truly become a distinctive trait of her personality and her philosophy of life. Some authors have maintained that her teaching on attention has been the main contribution of her life.[23]

Attention, Simone tells us, does not exist in physical effort, as many people think. It does not mean that our muscles tense or that our body goes rigid. It proceeds rather from a relaxation of all tensions, a laying aside of distractions, an opening of the interior faculties so that they are ready to receive truth. Attention means extricating oneself from all prejudice, waiting with expectancy, listening carefully, longing to penetrate reality as it really is, not as we may imagine it to be.

> Attention consists of suspending our thought, leaving it detached, empty and ready to be penetrated by the object. It means holding in our minds, within reach of this thought, but on a lower level and not in contact with it, the diverse knowledge we have acquired which we are forced to make use of. Our thought should be, in relation to all particular and already formulated thoughts, as a man on a mountain who, as he looks forward, sees also below him, without actually looking at them, a great many forests and plains. Above all, our thought should be empty, waiting, not seeking anything, but ready to receive in its naked truth the object which is to penetrate it.[24]

Simone did not apply this attitude only to abstract truth. Attention was a key concept for her in her relationships to people. We cannot really help others unless we first understand them as they see themselves, unless we give full attention to their unique personality. Few people have the charity to give another person such attention. Simone used to meditate endlessly on a line of the *Iliad* concerning the dead warriors who had been left unburied on the battlefield: "But they lay on the ground, dearer to the vultures than to their wives."[25] Most people, Simone reflected, love in the same way as they eat: They feed on other people. When they no longer find any use in a person, anything to feed on, they leave him or her to those who *can* still find something there to devour. The dead warriors received more attention from the vultures than from their wives whose love, presumably, had worn off.

> Those who are unhappy have no need for anything in this world but people capable of giving them their attention. The capacity to give one's attention to a sufferer is a very rare and difficult thing; it is almost a miracle; it *is* a miracle. Nearly all those who think they have this capacity do not possess it. Warmth of heart, impulsiveness, pity are not enough. . . .
>
> The love of our neighbor in all its fullness simply means being able to say to them: "What are you going through?" It is indispensable to know how to look at him in a certain way. This way of looking is first of all attentive. The soul empties itself of all its own contents in order to receive into itself the person it is looking at, just as he is, in all his truth. Only he who is capable of attention can do this.[26]

It was also through this same attitude of attention that Simone was open to receive her experience of Christ. Although she did not realize it at the time, her complete openness to truth in all its reality predisposed her for a person-to-person meeting with God. While she was attending the Holy Week ceremonies at Solesmes and listening with all her soul, and while she was reciting George Herbert's poem on "Love," she was, in fact, raising her mind to God by her attitude of attention. Later she realized this. She saw then that attention is the heart of prayer.

> The key to a christian conception of studies is the realization that prayer consists of attention. It is the orientation of all the attention of which the soul is capable towards God. The quality of the attention counts for much in the quality of the prayer. Warmth of heart cannot make up for it.
>
> It is the highest part of the attention only which makes contact with God, when prayer is intense and pure enough for such a contact to be established; but the whole attention is turned towards God.[27]

Simone, who was—let us not forget!—a teacher

herself, maintained that the highest value of education lies in its development of the faculty of attention. Even secular subjects such as mathematics, French and Greek can, if properly taught, train the mind toward attention. "All of them develop that faculty of attention which, directed towards God, is the very substance of prayer."[28]

Waiting for the Master

When Simone began to read and study the gospels, she was immediately attracted to them. One aspect of Christ's teaching that affected her deeply was the concept of "waiting in patience." Simone saw in it a confirmation of her own basic disposition. It was a discovery that moved her deeply. Father Perrin, who knew her personally for some time, narrates: "This insight was a very personal discovery for her. She rejoiced over it at Marseilles and talked to me about it. She remained excited about it in London and discussed it with Maurice Schumann."[29]

Christ spoke of different kinds of servants, Simone points out, and thereby he indicated different ways of service. There is the servant who works in the field and comes home after hard work. This servant is not invited to have his own meal; rather, he is made to do work again so that his master can eat first (Lk 17:7-10). But there is another kind of servant who waits for his master to come back. If the master finds him vigilant at his return, even when he comes at an unexpected hour, the master will reward him in a very personal way. He will make the servant sit at the table and will wait on him (Lk 12:35-37; cf. Mt 24:45-51). Not the working slave, but the slave who waits is the better model, says Simone.

> The slave who is to be loved is he who stands upright and motionless by the door in a state of watching, waiting, attention, desire — ready to open as soon as

he hears a knock. Neither weariness, nor hunger, nor the requests, the friendly invitations, the blows or jeers of his companions, nor the rumors which may be circulated round him to the effect that his master is dead or angry and determined to hurt him—nothing will disturb in slightest degree his attentive stillness.[30]

[Each student must strive to] be the slave—faithfully waiting while the master is absent, watching and listening—ready to open the door to him as soon as he knocks. The master will then make his slave sit down and himself serve him with meat. Only this waiting, this attention, can move the master to treat his slave with such amazing tenderness. . . . The thing which forces the master to make himself the slave of his slave, and to love him, has nothing to do with hard work. Still less is it the result of a search which the servant might have been bold enough to undertake on his own initiative. It is only watching, waiting, attention.[31]

A key word of the gospel in this context is the Greek term *hypomone*. The dictionary indicates as meanings: "patience," "endurance," "perseverance." The term is etymologically related to "waiting" (Greek: *hypomenein*) and cannot be so easily rendered in a modern language. Referring to the inadequacy of modern translations, Simone often prefers to use the Greek term itself, "that divinely beautiful expression of the Gospel." The following passages from the gospel thrilled her and had a special message for her (*hypomone* translated as "waiting in patience"):

"And as for [the seed that fell] in the good soil, they are those who, hearing the word, hold it fast in an honest and good heart, and bring forth fruit *waiting in patience*" (Lk 8:15,RSV).

"You will be hated by all for my name's sake. But he who *waits in patience* to the end will be saved" (Mt 10:22,RSV).

"By *waiting in patience* you will gain your lives" (Lk 21:19,RSV).

A New Kind of Saint

There are other realms of life in which Simone deserves to be our teacher. I am thinking especially of her wonderful discussions on Christian suffering. As few other spiritual writers of our day, she has penetrated the mystery of Christ's passion and grasped the paradoxical reality of a loving God who tolerates suffering. It convinced her of Christ's divinity. "The proof for me, the thing that is miraculous, is the perfect beauty of the accounts of the passion, together with some brief passages from Isaiah and St. Paul. That is what forces me to believe."[32]

What we may not pass over in this short account of Simone and her experience of the divine is her impassioned plea for a new kind of saint in the church.

> Today it is not nearly enough merely to be a saint, but we must have the saintliness demanded by the present moment, a new saintliness, itself without precedent. . . . I think that under this or any equivalent form it is the first thing we have to ask for now, we have to ask for it daily, hourly, like a famished child constantly asks for bread. The world needs saints who have genius, just as a plague-stricken town needs doctors.[33]

Was Simone such a saint herself? Perhaps, unconsciously she indicated through her life and convictions what kind of saint the world needs today.

It is useless to attempt a judgment on Simone's sanctity: As she is not likely to be canonized, such a judgment should be left to God alone. We should not make the mistake either of exaggerating her wisdom or taking all her statements as normative. Simone Weil repeatedly pointed out that her thoughts were often tentative and open to correction. "I do not know what they are worth." . . . "It is for others to decide what it is worth." . . . She would have been the last to ascribe absolute value to them.

Whatever else she was, Simone was certainly a

prophet, a spokesman for many outside the church, a true mystic and a witness for Christ. If we imitate her intellectual honesty, if we practice "attention" as she did, we will certainly come nearer to Christ. With Simone, we too may realize that "only God is worth the gift of our total attention and absolutely nothing else."[34] Attention and obedience to truth cannot fail to lead us to God.

> He (the divine Spirit) led me into a church (at Marseilles in 1942). It was new and ugly. He said to me, "Kneel down." I replied, "I have not been baptized." He said: "Fall on your knees before this place with love, as before the place where truth abides." I obeyed.[35]

Section III
You Need to Take Steps

Ten

Have Time for God

When the Syrian Naaman was told he would be cured of his leprosy by washing himself seven times in the river Jordan, he was disappointed. He had expected a more spectacular cure. Besides, what was so special about the Jordan? Surely, the rivers Abana and Pharpar, back in Damascus, were much better than any river in Israel! We know the reply he received from his assistants, "Sir, if the prophet had told you to do something difficult, you would have done it" (2 Kgs 5:13). Naaman's temptation is still ours today. Like him, we may be inclined to expect great things only from what is strange, unusual or outlandish. Often the best cure for our ills may be simple and ready at hand.

When we seek to have an experience of the Divine, when we want to be sensitive to the indwelling of the Holy Spirit and aware of Christ's life in us, we are not called upon to take extraordinary measures. We need not enroll in an expensive course or join an esoteric movement. We need not travel far in pilgrimage. We do not have to adopt another profession or effect drastic changes in our way of life. But one thing—simple enough in itself, but apparently more demanding than all those other things—is required: to set aside some time every day for silence, reflection and mental prayer.

Perhaps this requirement was less stringent in former ages when life proceeded at a more leisurely pace. In those days there were fewer distractions, fewer pressures of work, less noise. Most people were farmers or lived in the countryside; they were in close contact with nature. For thoughtful persons it was easier to find "slots" for withdrawal and interior recollection. In our own century the pace of life has quickened and tensions have increased. The work ethos spurs us on to restless activity, while modern technology fills our days with an unending stream of noise. To remain true to ourselves we have to refuse to be carried along by the maelstrom of trivialities. We have to build an island that we can call our own.

The remedy is setting aside 20 minutes to half-an-hour a day for silence and prayer. Within our day it should be an oasis, a period of peace, an experience we enjoy and look forward to. Making space for this practice should be possible for everyone. No single person can claim to be so busy, so involved or so distracted by legitimate concerns that he or she cannot manage to find this time. But, such is our swirling pattern of life these days, if we are not truly motivated and firmly determined in our resolve, we may well fail.

Oriental Wisdom

At this stage we may well turn to the religions of the East for enlightenment. They have developed many methods of reflection and contemplation. Practically all of them—Yoga, Taoism, Buddhism—originated in reaction to externalism in an age of empire building. Although these Oriental religions disagree considerably on the methods they recommend, what they have in common is that they prescribe withdrawal and silence.

The *Bhagavad-Gita* (possibly 500 B.C.) is a treatise on mysticism presented in the form of a conversation between Krishna, an incarnation of God, and Arjuna, a general. The background scene is a battlefield; the point is, obviously, that mysticism should flourish in the midst of an active life. Krishna gives the following advice:

"Day after day let the yogi practice the harmony of soul: in a secret place, in deep solitude, master of his mind, hoping for nothing, desiring nothing.

Let him find a place that is pure and a seat that is restful, neither too high nor too low, with sacred grass and a skin and a cloth thereon.

On that seat let him rest and practice yoga for the purification of the soul: with the life of his body and mind in peace; his soul in silence before the One.

With upright body, head and neck, which rest still and move not; with inner gaze which is not restless, but rests still between the eyebrows; with soul in peace, and all fear gone, and strong in the vow of holiness, let him rest with mind in harmony, his soul on me, his Lord supreme."[1]

When reading such a description our mind jumps at pictures of Indian saddhus or gurus whom we may have seen: cross-legged Indian ascetics sitting upright in obvious trance. But this is not what the *Bhagavad-Gita* had in mind. The book had been written for soldiers, administrators, shopkeepers; in other words, people like ourselves with occupations and distractions. Such persons are advised, not to abandon their professions, but to become "yogis" by taking time off for daily meditation. The advice applies equally well in our own circumstances and it is not surprising that many people today have taken to yoga.

One of the greatest Hindu leaders of Indian independence, Mahatma Gandhi, is an interesting, modern example of the ancient ideal. Although Gandhi led a very active life, he always remained a yogi at the same time. "Ever since my childhood," he tells us, "prayer has been my solace and my strength."[2] In all his disappointments, during periods of utmost darkness, at counsels of despair and counsels of caution, it was prayer that saved him. This was his experience "extending over an unbroken period of nearly forty years."[3]

Prayer has been the saving of my life. Without prayer I should have been a lunatic long ago. My autobiography will tell you that I have had my fair share of the bitterest public and private experiences. They threw me into temporary despair, but if I was able to get rid of it, it was because of prayer.[4]

For Gandhi, prayer was truly an interior communion with God. The essence of prayer was silence.

Silence has now become both a physical and spiritual necessity for me. Originally, it was taken to relieve the sense of pressure. Then I wanted time for writing. After, however, I had practiced it for some time I saw the spiritual value of it. It suddenly flashed across my mind that that was the time when I could best hold communion with God. And now I feel as though I was naturally built for silence. . . . I have often sought silence for communion even during my noisiest time. I have had recourse to sea voyages for this purpose, though, of course, the radio has now robbed even a sea voyage of the privilege of silence one used to enjoy on the boat. But silent prayer is not a monologue, but a dialogue, and God speaks to us only when we are silently ready to listen to him.[5]

It is not sufficiently realized how many of Gandhi's important decisions flowed from his interior prayer. Take the example of "*Satyagraha.*" This nonviolent resistance to British rule proved a very efficacious weapon in India's political struggle for independence. Gandhi was intelligent enough to evaluate its strength from a purely secular point of view. Yet, it would be a complete misunderstanding if its effectiveness were merely ascribed to Gandhi's astute way of wielding this new-found weapon. What made his nonviolence convincing was the unmistakable fact that it rested on a sincere desire for peace in spite of unavoidable conflict.

Gandhi resolved conflict through prayer. Two years before his assassination, he wrote:

Emptying the mind of all conscious processes of thought and filling it with the spirit of God unmanifest, brings one ineffable peace and attunes the soul with the

infinite. . . . . When the mind is completely filled with
His spirit, one cannot harbor ill-will or hatred towards
anyone, and, reciprocally, the enemy will shed his en-
mity and become a friend. It is not my claim that I have
always succeeded in converting enemies into friends,
but in numerous cases it has been my experience that
when the mind is filled with God's peace, all hatred
ceases.[6]

If great men like Gandhi saw the need for regular
silence and withdrawal, and if we can see how it
helped them to become spiritual persons, how much
more should we Christians adopt such a practice.[7]

Advice From a Saint

Earmarking time for silent prayer is, of course,
equally rooted in our own Christian tradition. Jesus
himself gave us the example. Withdrawing to lonely
places for reflection and prayer was his custom. If he
found no opportunity during the day, he would pray at
night. He would leave his disciples and go to a place
where he could be alone. "Jesus went up a hill to pray
and spent the whole night there praying to God" (Lk
6:12). "Crowds of people came to hear him and be
healed from their diseases. But he would go away to
lonely places, where he prayed" (Lk 5:15-16). "After
sending the people away, he went up a hill by himself
to pray. When evening came, Jesus was there alone"
(Mt 14:23). Jesus himself seems to have needed
moments when he was alone, away from the crowd,
face to face with his Father in silence.

Throughout the history of the church, spiritual
writers have stressed the importance of mental prayer
and saints have shown how it should be done in practice. Instead of adducing many such witnesses, I propose to introduce here one saintly teacher who brought
many people to an awareness of Christ. I am referring
to St. Francis de Sales (1567-1622), prince-bishop of

Geneva. In a time of great political and religious up-heaval, in many ways as turbulent as our own, this "gentleman saint" taught a mysticism that was within the reach of his flock.[8] His counsels were always practical and down to earth.

In the Middle Ages most spiritual exercises had been designed to fit the lives of priests and religious. De Sales rightly saw that this would not help his people. He would need to translate Christian ideals into a pattern of life that could be adopted by ordinary lay people. For this purpose he wrote a book, *Introduction to the Devout Life* (1608), a work entirely aimed at spelling out how responsible Catholics should practice their religion. Later he added his chief publication, *On the Love of God*. Many of the sermons and conferences he gave and personal letters written to individuals have also been preserved. What does Bishop de Sales say about our topic?

First of all, he always insists on the need for regularly setting time aside for prayer. We should carefully choose the best time of the day.

Spend an hour each day in meditation. Do this before lunch, if possible at the beginning of the morning when your mind is still less distracted and fresh after the night's rest. Do not give more than an hour to this. . . . If it happens that your whole morning passes without this exercise of mental prayer, either on account of many commitments or for some other reason—something which one should really never allow to happen!—then try to make up for the omission to the extent possible after lunch, at some opportune moment in the course of the afternoon. . . If you have not found an opportunity in the course of the whole day, you must make up for the loss by raising your mind more often to God in the course of your work, by taking up some spiritual reading and by imposing on yourself some penance to remind yourself of the seriousness of the omission. And don't forget to make a strong resolution to take up the practice again on the next day.[9]

In his private letters the bishop does not always prescribe the same length of time. To one married lady he says, "As to prayer, you should apply to it much; especially to meditation, for which you are, I think, well suited. Make then a short hour every day in the morning before going out, or else before the evening meal."[10] To quite a few others, men and women, married or widowed, he recommends, "Half an hour's prayer every morning—every day a good half-hour's spiritual reading."[11] The bishop explains that the length of time should depend partly on one's leisure and partly on the taste one has acquired. He advises one beginner to make her morning prayer "for a half quarter of an hour and even less."[12] To another he suggests, "Make your spiritual exercises short and fervent, that your natural disposition may not make prayer a difficulty to you on account of the length of it, and that little by little it may grow used to these acts of piety."[13] Never does he say that such prayer can be omitted. From all, he requires at least some regular time of meditation, normally lasting for at least half an hour.

In a letter to Madame de Chantal he speaks of his own practice:

> Yes, my child, by the grace of God I can say now better than before, that I make mental prayer, because I do not fail a single day in this; except sometimes on a Sunday, on account of confessions; and God gives me the strength to get up sometimes before daybreak for this purpose, when I foresee the multitude of the embarrassments of the day, and I do it all gaily; and meseems I have affection for it, and would greatly wish to be able to make it twice in the day; but it is not possible for me.[14]

The Where and the How

Francis de Sales also gives us advice as to how to spend the time. We should select a place where we are alone and at peace; we should deliberately seek solitude and silence.

> You should also take a liking to real, physical solitude. I don't mean that you need to go out into the desert as the old hermits did. . . .It will be enough to stay in your room or walk in your garden or remain in any other place where you find it easy to recollect yourself. There you should withdraw your mind within your own heart and refresh yourself with some solid reflection, some holy thoughts or some useful reading.[15]

To help his clients the bishop suggests that one could follow these five steps: putting oneself in the presence of God; asking God for help; reading a part of scripture and thinking about it with the mind and the imagination; responding to the mystery contained in it by sentiments and acts of the will; formulating a final conclusion. It is good, he says, to prepare carefully and to follow such a procedure. It will help us enter into the spirit of meditation and make a good start. But at no time should we think that such a method is an end in itself. It should be abandoned as soon as we achieve our real purpose, which is communion with God in mind and heart.

> It may sometimes happen that immediately after the preparation you will find your heart moved in God. Then you should let yourself go, without wanting to follow the method I suggested. . . . This is a general rule that you should never hold back your emotions, you should give them free rein whenever they present themselves. This is also true for other feelings, such as wanting to give thanks, wanting to offer yourself to God or to make petitions.[16]

> Practice prayer either by points, as I have said, or after your own custom, it matters little: but I distinctly remember telling you just to prepare the points, and to

try at the beginning of prayer to relish them; if you relish them it is a sign that at least for that time, God wants you to follow this method. If, however, the sweet customary presence (of God) engages you afterwards, entertain it; enter also into the familiar discussion which God himself suggests, and which, as you explained them to me in your letter, are good. . . . Go simply, sincerely, frankly, and with the simplicity of children, sometimes in the arms of the heavenly Father, sometimes holding his hand.[17]

Do not torment yourself about your prayer, which you say is without words; for it is good, if it leaves good effects in your heart. Do not force yourself to speak in this divine love; he speaks in us who looks and is seen. Follow, then, the path into which the Holy Ghost draws you, though I do not wish you to give up preparing yourself for meditation, as you used to do at the beginning. This you owe on your side, and you should of yourself take no other way; but when you intend to put yourself in it, if God draws you into another, go with him into it; we must on our side make a preparation according to our measure, and when God carries us higher, to him alone be the glory of it.[18]

Remaining in God's Presence

The bishop teaches that it is a grave mistake to imagine that our meditation is like a job we have to do, like hard work of which we should see the fruits. This would be an altogether wrong starting point. No, we should from the outset think of our recollection as merely being in the presence of God, of being at his service. He has some interesting things to say about what it means to put oneself in the presence of God and to stay there:

To *keep* ourselves in the presence of God, and to *place* ourselves in the presence of God, are, in my opinion, two things: for, to place ourselves there it is necessary to recall our minds from every other object, and to make it attentive to this presence actually, as I say in my book; but after placing ourselves, we keep ourselves there so long as we make, either by understanding or by will, acts towards God, whether by looking at him, or looking at some other thing for love of him; or looking at nothing, but speaking to him; or, neither looking nor speaking, but simply staying where he has put us, like a statue in its niche.[19]

We put ourselves in God's presence to give him the honor and homage we owe him; and this can be done without his speaking to us or we to him: for this duty is paid by remembering that he is our God, and we his vile creatures, and by remaining prostrate in spirit before him, awaiting his commands. How many courtiers go a hundred times into the presence of the king, not to hear him or speak to him, but simply to be seen by him, and to testify by this assiduity that they are his servants?[20]

The expectation, then, we should have of our time of recollection, what we should try to achieve, is nothing more nor less than being attentive (at attention) in God's presence. If God wishes, he will act on us in his own good time. Our duty consists in withdrawing ourselves from other attachments, in making ourselves free and available to him. We make ourselves vulnerable and then wait in a relaxed and joyful manner.

You do nothing, you say, in prayer. But what would you do, except what you do, which is to present and represent to God your nothingness and your misery? It is the best plea beggars make us when they expose to our sight their ulcers and needs.

But sometimes again you do nothing of all this, as you tell me, but remain there like a phantom or a statue. Well, and that is not a little thing. In the palaces of princes and kings, statues are put which are only of use to gratify the prince's eyes; be satisfied then with serving for that purpose, in the presence of God; he will give life to this statue when he likes.

Trees only bear fruit through the presence of the sun, some sooner, others later, some every year, and others every three years, and not always equally. While being happy to be able to stay in the presence of God, let us be assured that he will make us bear our fruit, sooner or later, always or sometimes, according to his good pleasure, to which we must entirely resign ourselves.[21]

Making a Retreat

Our practice of daily meditation will be greatly strengthened if at times we grant ourselves the opportunity of making a retreat. Many Christians know from experience what a retreat can mean; many others may never have taken it up. Even for those who know and appreciate retreats it may be helpful to reflect once more on what a retreat is meant to do and how it can achieve its purpose.

The essence of a retreat is our withdrawal from everyday life and all its involvements for a considerable amount of time. We go for a number of days to some other place where we shall not be distracted from our main task in hand: sorting ourselves out in the face of God.

We should select the place carefully. It should be such that it allows us to be fully cut off from our work, our family, the news and other business that normally commands our attention. We withdraw to a place where we can be free from attending to such matters, not because we want to escape responsibility for them, but because we know that having reaffirmed our relationship to God we shall be able to discharge our duties better. The place where we make our retreat should be friendly, not too austere, affording us a maximum of spiritual freedom. Sometimes a convent or monastery may lend itself to the purpose; at other times we may simply stay with friends who have promised to leave us alone.

In some countries the only retreat that is widely

known is the so-called *directed* retreat. In such a retreat a group of people come together, usually in a special retreat house, to follow a program of daily talks and spiritual exercises. The advantage of this arrangement is the availability of an experienced retreat master. Through his sermons and personal guidance the retreat father can help us focus attention on aspects of our spiritual life that we may consciously or unconsciously have neglected. A directed retreat also provides updated information which makes it of special value for people who have little chance of keeping themselves informed about what is happening in the church.

However, there are also drawbacks to such a retreat. The spiritual input may be overloaded, with too many topics introduced, too many items on the timetable. The retreat is then in danger of becoming a training course, profitable no doubt, but no longer a "retreat." Since the program is planned for the average person and addressed to groups, it may not respond to the needs of a particular individual. Moreover, there are other limiting factors in organized retreats, such as convenient dates, accommodation, etc., that may well restrict its usefulness in some cases.

That is why I should like to point out that the normal and perhaps best retreat we can make is one which we plan ourselves. Taking a few days off for our spiritual life should be possible and normal for almost anyone. Half a century ago, going away on a vacation was unthinkable for most; improved working conditions and a better living standard have brought it within reach of most people. Similarly, without too much inconvenience, it should be possible for individuals or married couples to arrange their own "retreat" in a convenient place.

How long should a retreat last? Obviously, no hard and fast rules can be given. Much can be achieved in three full days of silence and seclusion. But personally

I am more in favor of a six- or eight-day retreat, if it is at all possible. Experience shows that we need one or two days to set aside our immediate involvements, one or two days spent in gradually coming to rest and getting the taste of higher things. There are processes in life that we cannot speed up and this seems to be one of them. A horse that has been running a race is all steamed up and requires time and rest to gain its composure. Without knowing it, we, too, are mentally and emotionally so engrossed in external concerns that we require a few days to gradually let these anchors go. In a six-day retreat it is usually the fourth and the fifth days that give us the most peace and the deepest contact with God. However much we try not to, on the last day we shall be preparing ourselves to return to our normal engagements.

The essence of a retreat is what Benedictines used to call "*Vacare Deo*," that is, making oneself empty for God. We should not put ourselves under any kind of pressure. We should feel free and happy. Much of our time will be spent in leisure, walking around in a park or doing something else that sets our mind free. When we are ready for it, we may give ourselves some spiritual nourishment, possibly by a combination of reading from scripture and from a book that seems relevant to us. It is interesting to note that on the Mount of Transfiguration the Law and the prophets were present in their protagonists, Moses and Elijah.

While allowing ourselves a maximum amount of freedom, we should from the start put Christ at the center of our retreat. We should remind ourselves continuously of his presence. We should make up our minds that we don't want to do anything without him. We should feel a great desire to get to know him intimately. We should ask him to guide and help us at every stage. We should see the whole of our retreat basically as prayer in the widest sense of the word, a gradual opening of ourselves to all that Christ is. Our fundamental attitude might well be expressed in words such as these which we repeat from time to time:

> "Dear Jesus, I have come to sort myself out. Please, accept me as I am with all my contradictory aspirations. What I desire most of all is to be true to myself, to what you want me to be. I know that union with you will be my highest fulfillment. I admire you, Jesus, I adore you and accept you as my only master. Please, be with me during these days in a special way, speak to me, fill my heart with your presence. Help me to come closer to you during this retreat. With all my heart I want to know and love you better."

Should we make the retreat alone or in the company of others? It all depends. Discussions with others can be fruitful, but too much discussion destroys the seclusion and silence that are the main characteristics of a real retreat. However, if doing a retreat with others safeguards the individual's time of solitary prayer, if it means that occasionally we come together for common prayer, or for a prayerful exchange of our thoughts and experiences, then such an arrangement may, indeed, be a help. In fact, for married couples or for pastoral teams or for others engaged in the same type of work, such mutual support in prayer and reflection may deepen one's own experience. However, we should be aware of the danger that all too readily we may again be absorbed in dealing with other people rather than making ourselves empty for God. The retreat should make us free and available for Christ.

In the strict sense of the term there is, of course, no guarantee that during a retreat we will have a peak experience such as Peter, James and John had on Mount Tabor. Such events are not within our control. Yet we may not exclude the possibility either. If we make an effort to be really free and available, Christ in his own time and at his own good pleasure, will not fail to make his presence felt. In some unexpected way he will reveal himself to us. His dazzling light will burn an indelible mark in us. Christ will not fail us.

Practical Conclusions

If we have not adopted the practice already, we should resolve to set aside *every day* a definite period of time for silence and mental prayer. For this we should choose a place where we are free and relaxed, where we shall not be disturbed by others. We make this withdrawal a "sacred hour"; we make up for it when, for one reason or other, we have missed our usual time.

After putting ourselves in the presence of God, we make a short, spontaneous introductory prayer. We then turn our thoughts to a passage of Sacred Scripture, to a book we are reading or to another spiritual input of the same kind. We do not try to force results. Rather, in a spirit of love and resignation we keep ourselves consciously in God's presence.

Once a year, or once every so many years, we make a retreat which we consider to be a vacation in God's presence.

In one of his sarcastic essays C. Northcote Parkinson introduces what he calls the "Law of Triviality." Finance committees are inclined to pass expenditure involving millions of dollars in a short time, but will spend hours discussing the outlay of a few dollars. "Briefly stated, the Law of Triviality means that the time spent on any item of the agenda will be in inverse proportion to the sum involved."[22] Having time for God is a start in recognizing where our real treasure lies. It liberates us from the Law of Triviality. It makes us invest time where it borders on eternity.

Eleven
Internalize Scripture

Christ will show himself to us if we keep his word. He remains present to us through his Spirit and his word. Sacred Scripture, particularly the gospels, play a central part in joining us in mind and heart to Christ.

How should we know scripture? The thought might come to us that scripture scholars know the text best and should, therefore, be closest to Christ. But the absurdity of this thought becomes immediately apparent. For it is perfectly possible—unfortunately!—for someone to possess a thorough scientific knowledge of scripture without even being a Christian. A university professor may be able to read the original text in Hebrew or Greek, be familiar with the commentaries and master the contents of the inspired message. Yet he may well lack faith and teach scripture as someone else might teach the Dammapada of the Buddhists. A good scientific knowledge of scripture may be a help, but it does not in itself suffice. A totally different kind of knowledge is required.

To bear fruit, the words of scripture must be received with faith and love and should be internalized. This means that they should become part and parcel of our own thinking. It is obviously not possible for anyone to internalize the whole of scripture; nor is it necessary. For each individual certain parts of scripture are more relevant than others. Internalizing is greatly aided by a cultivation of such texts. Usually such key elements of the message are best digested by us in the form of "images."

Jesus and the Old Law

To understand what internalizing means and how it works, what better example could we find than the one given by our Lord himself? Although Jesus was the Son of God and as such all-knowing from eternity, he did not choose this omniscience as the foundation of his human thinking. Becoming a man in all respects, except for sin, he wanted to grow in wisdom, to learn and build up his own thought patterns as all of us do. Jesus received the instruction other children received in his time. He imbibed the culture of his own people. His religious concepts and feelings were nourished, like those of his contemporaries, by the Old Testament. As Jesus matured, he sifted all the information and, in prayer and meditation, worked out the religious constructs we now find in the gospels.

Allow me to illustrate this process by an example. When Exodus narrates Israel's lapse from God by the adoration of the golden calf, it mentions that only the tribe of Levi remained loyal to Yahweh. To stop the idolatry, Moses called on the Levites to punish all those who were guilty, even if they were relatives or close friends. "The LORD God of Israel commands every one of you to put on your sword and go through the camp from this gate to the other and kill your brothers, your friends, and your neighbors" (Ex 32:27). They obeyed and received a special blessing: "Today you have consecrated yourselves as priests in the service of the LORD by killing your sons and brothers" (Ex 32:29). In the litany of blessings over individual tribes, which Moses is said to have spoken before his death, he once more praised the Levites for what they had done:

> "They showed greater loyalty to you
> Than to parents, brothers, or children.
> They obeyed your commands
> And were faithful to your covenant" (Dt 33:9).

Experiencing Jesus
156

These Old Testament texts made a deep impression on Jesus. In his imagination he must have pictured to himself what a horrible plight the Levites found themselves in. Some of their close relatives had turned away from God and were misleading the people. Loyalty to God demanded that they be ruthless and turn against those closely related to them by family ties. Jesus would also have remembered the warning in Deuteronomy 13:6-8: "Even your brother or your son or your daughter or the wife you love or your closest friend may secretly encourage you to worship other gods, gods that you and your ancestors have never worshiped. . . . Do not let him persuade you; do not even listen to him. Show him no mercy or pity, and do not protect him." Jesus would have recalled Micah's bitter complaint, "In these times sons treat their fathers like fools, daughters oppose their mothers, and young women quarrel with their mothers-in-law; a man's enemies are the members of his own family" (Mi 7:6).

I imagine Jesus meditating about these words in Nazareth, allowing them to sink in while strolling around on a Sabbath or while engaged in his carpenter's job. There were certain aspects of the old tradition that Jesus deliberately discarded. He did not believe his Father would want to restore a priestly order such as that held by the Levites. Neither would he ever dream of killing other persons in punishment for unbelief. But one particular implication of the inspired words, in fact the core of their message, moved him deeply and shaped his future thinking. He would never allow family ties or bonds of friendship to stand in the way of loyalty to his Father! He steeled himself to be, in this regard, as ruthless and unrelenting as the Levites had been. The incident in the Temple related in Luke 2:41-50 may well be an indication that Jesus went through this process when he was about 12 years old. Even at that early age he had made up his mind to attend first and foremost to his Father's business.

Understanding Jesus' decision, we appreciate better some of his seemingly harsh statements. When someone praised his mother, "How happy is the woman who bore you and nursed you!" Jesus replied, "Rather, how happy are those who hear the word of God and obey it!" (Lk 11:27-28). When somebody told him, "Your mother and brothers are standing outside, and they want to speak with you," Jesus answered, "Whoever does what my Father in heaven wants him to do, is my brother, my sister, and my mother" (Mt 12:46-50). In other words, loyalty to God is more important than family relationships. Although Jesus loved his mother (Jn 19:25-27), although he never minimized the duty of respecting one's parents (Mt 15:4-6; 19:19), he saw love of God as a higher duty.

Consistency

Jesus demanded an equally strict attitude of his disciples. He said to a certain person, "Follow me." When the man asked permission to go back and bury his father first, Jesus retorted: "Let the dead bury their own dead. You go and proclaim the Kingdom of God" (Lk 9:60). And to the man who wanted to say goodbye to his family, Jesus said, "anyone who starts to plow and then keeps looking back is of no use for the Kingdom of God" (Lk 9:62). Following Jesus implies the fundamental readiness to leave "brothers, sisters, father, mother or children" (Mt 19:29).

At the Last Supper Jesus said to his disciples, "Peace is what I leave with you; it is my own peace that I give you" (Jn 14:27). Jesus was referring to the peace of conscience, to the peace that fills our hearts when we let our lives be ruled by his love. But he does not bring peace if by "peace" we mean lack of opposition. No, his radical demands will cause many people to reject and hate us. Jesus came to bring the sword of the Levites, the sword of loyalty to God rather than to one's family.

> "Do not think that I have come to bring peace to the world. No, I did not come to bring peace, but a sword. I came to set sons against their fathers, daughters against their mothers, daughters-in-law against their mothers-in-law; a man's worst enemies will be the members of his own family.
>
> "Whoever loves his father or mother more than me is not fit to be my disciple; whoever loves his son or daughter more than me is not fit to be my disciple" (Mt 10:34-37).

Jesus' thoughts are rooted in the Old Testament texts, but they have outgrown them. What the Old Testament really wanted to imprint, the need for loyalty to God above everything else, had become Jesus' own. He took this principle and refashioned it so that it could become an integral part of his doctrine and life. It had become so much part of his whole approach that in unexpected circumstances he reacted spontaneously in harmony with it. He quoted it implicitly in many things he thought and said. Jesus had "internalized" this important part of the Old Testament message.

The Process

Many other aspects of Jesus' mental make-up could be analyzed in a similar way. We always find that both elements are present: a permeating influence of the inspired Word and an entirely original manner in which Jesus understood and realized it. This is, I believe, the pattern according to which we too should internalize the word of scripture, particularly Jesus' own word. We should allow the text to speak to us, and when a part of the message strikes us as particularly relevant, we should work out its implications in detail and integrate it into our whole thinking and living. What counts is not the number of texts we know, but the depth of our adhesion to certain texts and their transforming effect in our lives.

Francis of Assisi modeled his entire life on Jesus' injunction, "Don't take anything with you on the trip . . . "(Mk 6:7). Jesus' teaching on poverty permeated all his thinking and guided his decisions. We can truly say that Francis "internalized" that part of the gospel. It became for him the key by which he could open many doors into Jesus' message. It was his anchor in the gospels. Francis achieved his greatness by fully responding to this highly individual appeal the gospel had for him. This is the way internalization works.

When reading scripture, we should not try to cover everything. Rather, we should pay special attention to those texts that seem to have meaning for us personally. We should make a treasury of such texts in the sense that we frequently think about them, and that we study them with preference. When we face Christ in our periods of silence and meditation, it will be particularly from these texts that we begin our prayerful reflection. We should make the message of these texts penetrate the marrow of our bones. We should reformulate them in our own words and translate them into action. In this way we can make the inspired Word our own, with the same intensity and freedom displayed by Jesus.

Symbols and Images

As the mind is our highest faculty, we might be tempted to think that concepts, ideas and thoughts are the strongest ingredients of our inner personality. Psychology has shown that this is not the case. It is impossible for us to think in purely rational terms. We always employ visual images as well, and respond with our emotions. In fact, symbols and images prove to be our most powerful means of clarifying thought and building up personality.

The image of "territory" is common to animals as

well as human beings. We think of it as a place belonging to us with well-defined boundaries (the territorial imperative). We need the image not only for such everyday, physical notions as "home," "neighbor," and so on, but also when describing about abstract realities. The image of territorial rights is implicit in notions such as freedom of religion (my religious beliefs are within my territory), juridical competence (what are the limits of his territory?) and medical specializations (only certain diseases are within my territory). When we say it is difficult for people to be saved "outside the church," we are considering the community of the faithful as a territory with clear boundaries. We should also notice that the image of territory evokes an emotional response; in our own territory we feel at home, safe and happy. It helps clarity of thinking to recognize such images explicity.

One way of internalizing scripture is by adopting some of its images. Again, we find some good examples in the life of Christ. Take, for instance, the Old Testament custom of having a year of "release" every seventh year. The Law of Moses prescribed that every seventh year was to be considered a holy year, a year of the Lord. At the beginning of this year, citizens who had been forced to sell themselves as slaves had to be set free and all debts were canceled (Dt 15:1-18). This holy year of God, when slaves and poor people were released, became in the Isaian prophecies an image of the future, messianic liberation:

> The Sovereign LORD has filled me with this spirit.
> He has chosen me and sent me
> To bring good news to the poor,
> To heal the broken-hearted,
> To announce release to captives
> And freedom to those in prison (Is 61:1).

It was an image Jesus took to with all his heart. When he preached in Nazareth it was this passage he selected to express his own task (Lk 4:16-21). Jesus saw himself as heralding this year of release, the new era when salvation would be brought to all captives of sin and evil.

Jesus had worked out some consequences of this image. The year of release obliged all men to forgive one another's debts. This would be a constant theme of his preaching. Because God has granted a general release, we too should cancel all debts. The parable of the unforgiving servant is based on this conviction (Mt 18:21-35). Jesus builds it into the Our Father as an essential element of our relationship to God (Mt 6:12-15; Mk 11:25). We should notice particularly that, when speaking of forgiving our neighbors' *sins,* Jesus calls them "debts," thereby deliberately harking back to the image of remitting debts during the year of release.

It was not the wealthy who rejoiced when the year of release came round, but the poor. It was good news especially for underdogs and slaves. With this in mind Jesus can say, "Happy are you poor; the Kingdom of God is yours!" (Lk 6:20). It makes Jesus go out of his way to meet tax collectors and other public sinners. "I have not come to call respectable people, but outcasts" (Mt 9:13). The kingdom of God is biased toward those who are most in need. "There will be more joy in heaven over one sinner who repents than over ninety-nine respectable people who do not need to repent" (Lk 15:7).

In all this we have again an example of how Jesus internalized the inspired message of the Old Testament. He took the image of the year of release as a guiding principle to rule his own ideas on the kingdom of his Father. We may be sure that long before starting his public life, Jesus had absorbed this image in continuous reflection and prayer. Perhaps, with a good amount of poetic licence, we might reconstruct Jesus' thoughts in this way:

What a joy, what happiness there must have been among the slaves and the very poor when the year of release was announced! There must have been great rejoicing and dancing when messengers traveled through the length and breadth of the land, proclaiming that the year of the Lord had started!

Yes, this is what it will be like when the kingdom of my Father is announced. It shall be a kingdom of release, release of sins, total forgiveness on the part of God for all those who humble themselves. There will be great joy and happiness for small people, for those who are ignorant and cannot help themselves. No longer shall there be any inequality or discrimination. Every human being will have the chance of becoming a child of God.

If this was the way Jesus built up his own self-understanding and doctrine, we should not underestimate the great role of images in our own lives. It is certain that we operate with such images, but it may well be that we have never consciously adverted to them. Recognizing the images that motivate us and consciously enriching them with biblical images is a very powerful way of internalizing scripture. We find this confirmed in the lives of the saints.

We saw earlier that the meeting between Jesus and the Samaritan woman exerted a great attraction on Teresa of Avila. It was literally an "image" too in the sense that Teresa kept it alive by having a painting of the incident at hand. The image helped Teresa at different stages of her life to understand her relationship to Christ. In the beginning she was intrigued by the meeting itself (*What a thrill if Jesus would meet me in such a way!*), then her attention was focused on the water Jesus promised (*Lord, give me such water to drink!*). Later she took courage from the Samaritan woman's apostolate in Sychar (*If she being a sinner could do so much, there is also hope for me.*). Teresa benefited very much from her outspoken preference for this biblical image.

Symeon of Constantinople worked with a different image. He had been struck by the phrase, "God is light." Not only did the concepts of light and darkness put their stamp on many of his theological terms, but he was so full of the image that he perceived God's presence as a form of inner light.

Thérèse of Lisieux made use of many images, partly based on her own experience, partly derived from scripture. She was "the little flower" growing in Jesus' garden. She was the child carried in God's arms, the ship sailing on God's ocean, the swallow lifted by the eagle. Thérèse relished such images and used them with great insight as the pillars and supporting beams of her spiritual edifice.

Loving Response

In the foregoing section I drew attention to the fact that we can never think without somehow involving our emotions. I must admit, however, that there is a real danger of intellectualism for some persons. By natural disposition or by the training they have received, they are inclined to think that faith and prayer move mainly in the field of knowledge and the mind. Their approach to meditation may be predominantly notional. They may labor under the impression that prayer means thinking about God or addressing our thoughts to God.

Although thinking is a necessary preparation, union with God comes through love. "Whoever accepts my commandments and obeys them is the one who loves me. My Father will love whoever loves me; I too will love him and reveal myself to him" (Jn 14:21). Accepting Jesus' word is not a notional assent; it is a loving acceptance of Jesus himself!

Internalizing scripture involves such a loving response. When Jesus decided to be loyal to his Father as the Levites had been, it was a resolve of his heart. When he evolved the image of the messianic year of release, he did so with his heart full of hope and joyful expectation. We can only speak of true internalization if the message has been anchored in our will and our emotions as much as in our intellect.

Putting It All Together

When we make our regular meditation, as described in the previous chapter, we should use Sacred Scripture as our chief source. In doing this, however, we are not concerned with completing a certain number of verses, but with deepening our understanding and love.

It may be that a certain passage has struck us forcibly. We should then not leave that passage without having exhausted all the riches it can offer, even if it takes us many successive meditations to do so. We might compare the text with other scriptural passages or read commentaries or articles that enlighten it. If it contains an image that appeals to us, we may spend much time in working it out and accepting it with all our being. We examine our actual behavior to see if it corresponds to the implications of the text, and we ask God repeatedly to open our hearts so that we may respond fully to his word.

If we spend a considerable amount of time and prayer on such texts, we shall soon have a treasury of favorite passages. We may underline them in our bible or mark them in the margin. They may be the texts we turn to with preference in moments of despondency. They will often provide an easy launching pad for a deeply personal exchange of love with God.

There are periods when we feel that we are not particularly kindled by any special text, and so we break new ground by turning to another passage or reading another book. At all times, however, we should remember that we are in the presence of God and that we have not come to seek profound thoughts or speak beautiful words. Our first duty is to love and serve him with all our heart. So at any time we should give precedence to spontaneous prayers that well up from within us. And we should be quite content to remain in God's presence in loving silence. After all, it is not words that count but the love of the heart.

Footnotes

Chapter One: Jesus' Promise

1. B. Lindars, *The Gospel of John,* New Century Bible (London: Oliphants, 1972), p. 482.

2. J. H. Bernard, *A Critical and Exegetical Commentary on the Gospel According to St. John,* A. H. McNeile, ed. (Edinburgh: Clark, 1928), p. 550.

3. "Jesus will unite himself more intimately and personally with his disciples so that his return will be a source of greater individual sanctity. . . . While taking leave from them as far as the body is concerned, he promises to return in a mystical fashion. . . . Just as Jesus' return is a spiritual event, so 'the seeing' of him by the disciples will be an interior event realized through faith and love."

   J. Keulers, *Het Evangelie volgens Johannes* (Roermond: Romen en Zonen, 1951), p. 262.

4. Brown continues: "This does not mean that passages such as this strip the Easter event of its external, miraculous character (Bultmann, p. 479), and that there is no difference between post-resurrectional appearances and indwelling. Rather the Fourth Gospel (20:27) goes out of its way to insist on the external character of the appearances and the bodily reality of the risen Jesus. But John has also realized that the appearances are not an end in themselves; they initiate and point to a deeper kind of presence. . . .

   "It should be noted that none of these passages is concerned with the presence of Jesus encountered by mystics; the presence of Jesus is promised, not to an ascetical elite, but to Christians in general."

   R. E. Brown, *The Gospel According to John,* Anchor Bible (London: Chapman, 1966), p. 646.

5. A. Wikenhauser, *Het Evangelie volgens Johannes* (Antwerp: Patmos, 1964), p. 337.

6. Thomas Aquinas, *Summa Theologica*, 1 q.8, a.3.

7. Ibid., 1 q.43, a.3.

Chapter Two: Jesus' Word and Jesus' Spirit

1. W. Grundmann, *Evangelium nach Markus* (Berlin, 1959), p. 8.

2. I am following here the alternative translation indicated in:
   R. E. Brown, *The Gospel According to John*, Vol. 1, Anchor Bible (London: Chapman, 1966), pp. 320-322.
   Brown himself prefers a translation that would imply that the rivers of living water flow from *Jesus* rather than from the believer. Even if this interpretation is followed, the overall message remains the same.

3. Ibid., p. 321.

4. K. V. Truhlar, "Report of a Pilgrim," 4, *Christus Erfahrung* (Rome: Herder, 1964); here in the Dutch translation, Paul Brand (Hilversum, 1965), p. 41.

5. Ibid., p. 40.

6. R. E. Brown, "The Holy Spirit in the Fourth Gospel," *The Expositor* (1925), pp. 292-299.

Chapter Three: Scripture and Radiance

1. Scriptural references in serial order: Jn 6:68; 17:17; 14:24; 6:63; 12:48; 8:34; 5:24; 4:50; 2:22; 4:41; 12:48; 8:51; 8:43; 15:20; 5:38; 8:37; 8:31; Mk 8:38; Lk 11:28; Mt 24:35.

2. H. Schuermann, "Die vorösterlichen Anfänge der Logientradition," *Der Historische Jesus and Kerugmatische Christus*, ed. H. Ristow and K. Matthiae (Berlin: Evangelische Verlagsanstalt, 1962), pp. 342-370.

3. Cf. the so-called "persecution form," a set of warnings and instructions that recur in the New Testament writings:
   E.G. Selwyn, *The First Epistle to St. Peter*, Essay II (London, 1946), pp. 441ff.

4. K. Rahner, *Inspiration in the Bible* (London, 1964), pp. 40-57.

5. Ibid., pp. 53ff.

6. Cf. J.N.M. Wijngaards, "Christian Radiance," *Mission Spirituality,* ed. C. Srambical (Indore: Divine Word Publications, 1976), pp. 52-69.

7. G. Von Rad, "Kabód in the Old Testament," *Theological Dictionary of the New Testament,* ed. R. Kittel, Vol. II (Grand Rapids: Eerdmans, 1964), pp. 238-242.

8. Ibid.

Chapter Four: Symeon the New Theologian

1. G. A. Maloney, *The Mystic of Fire and Light* (Denville: Dimension Books, 1975), pp. 31-35. Most of the information contained in this chapter derives from this book.

2. Ibid., pp. 15,29.

3. Ibid., pp. 61, 37, 49, 58, 67.

4. Ibid., pp. 57-58, 73, 49, 68.

5. Ibid., pp. 101-104 (I have attempted to "modernize" the English, adapting expressions and diction to present-day usage).

Chapter Five: Thérèse of Lisieux

1. B. Bro, "Een heilige voor onze tijd," *Internationale Katholieke Informatie* 7 (1973), August, pp. 16-22.

2. Thérèse of Lisieux, *The Story of a Soul*, trans. G. M. Day (London: Burns & Oates, 1951), p. 123.

3. Bro, op. cit., p. 18.

4. *The Story of a Soul,* p. 140.

5. From a letter to a missionary;
P. Liagre, *A Retreat with St. Thérèse* (Dublin: Gill, 1959), p. 10.

6. *The Story of a Soul,* pp. 129-130.

7. D. Bannister and F. Fransella, *Inquiring Man* (Penguin, 1971).

8. *The Story of a Soul,* p. 74.

9. Ibid., p. 75.

10. Ibid., p. 102.

11. Ibid., p. 120.

12. Ibid., p. 61.

13. Ibid., p. 27.

14. Ibid., p. 73.

15. Ibid., p. 6.

16. Ibid.

17. Ibid., Cant 2:1, p. 53.

18. Ibid., pp. 94-95.

19. Ibid., pp. 157-158.

20. Ibid., p. 183.

21. Ibid., p. 187.

22. Ibid., pp. 135-136. The quotations are from Proverbs 9:4 and Isaiah 66:12-13.

23. Ibid., pp. 183-184.

24. Ibid., p. 78.

25. Ibid., p. 99.

26. Ibid., p. 194.

27. Ibid., p. 56.

28. Ibid., p. 154.

29. Ibid., pp. 194-195.

30. Ibid., p. 155.

31. Cf. J.N.M. Wijngaards, *Communicating the Word of God* (Great Wakering: Mayhew-McCrimmon, 1978), pp. 236-238.
This aspect of Thérèse's life has been treated extensively by: I.F. Goerres, *The Hidden Face* (New York: Pantheon, 1959).

Chapter Six: Francis of Assisi

Throughout this chapter *The Little Flowers of St. Francis* (Flowers), *The Mirror of Perfection* (Mirror), and St. Bonaventure's *Life of St. Francis* (Life) will be quoted from their one-volume edition in Everyman's Library (London: Dent, 1973; originally London, 1910).

1. *Life,* Ch. IV, Par. 1, p. 322.

2. *Flowers,* Ch. XVI, pp. 28-29.

3. *Mirror,* Ch. XXVI, pp. 205-206.

4. Ibid.

5. *Life,* Ch. III, Par. 1, p. 316.

6. J. Joergensen, *St. Francis of Assisi* (New York: Image Book, 1955), p. 57. The first edition was published in 1911.

7. *Mirror,* Ch. LXXVI, p. 251.

8. Thomas Von Celano, *Leben und Wunder des heiligen Franziskus von Assisi,* ed. Werl, 1962, II, Ch. LXXI; quoted in W. Egger, "Den Herrn in den Schriften Suchen," *Bibel und Kirche* 4 (1976), pp. 122-125.

9. *Mirror,* Ch. XXXVIII, p. 215.

10. Ibid., Ch. IV, pp. 187-188.

11. Ibid., Ch. LXIX, p. 243.

12. *Life,* Ch. XI, p. 369.

13. Ibid., Ch. III, Par. 8, pp. 319-320.

Chapter Seven: Charles de Foucauld

1. J.F. Six, *Spiritual Autobiography of Charles de Foucauld* (Denville: Dimension Books, 1964), p. 147.

2. Ibid., p. 20.
   For further extracts of letters in which he develops this thought, cf. G. Gorree, *Memories of Charles de Foucauld* (London: Burns, Oates & Washbourne, 1938), pp. 35-46.

3. Ibid., p. 48.

4. Ibid., p. 50.

5. Ibid., pp. 61-62 (translation slightly adapted).

6. Ibid., pp. 82-83.

7. Ibid., p. 33.

8. Ibid., p. 19.

9. Ibid., pp. 22, 16, 100, 10, 108.

10. Ibid., p. 87.

11. Ibid., pp. 73-77.

Chapter Eight: Teresa of Avila

1. Teresa of Avila, *Life*, Ch. 10; E. Allison Peers, *The Complete Works of Saint Teresa of Jesus,* Vol. I (London: Sheed and Ward, 1946), p. 61.

2. E. Hamilton, *The Great Teresa* (London: Catholic Book Club, 1960), p. 30.

3. Ibid., pp. 21, 26, 32.

4. *Life*, Ch. 30; Peers, op. cit., p. 203.

5. Teresa of Avila, *Soliloquies* 9, 2; K. Kavanaugh and O. Rodrigues, *The Collected Works of St. Teresa of Avila,* Vol. I (Washington: ICS, 1976), p. 382.

6. *Spiritual Testimony* 26; Kavanaugh and Rodrigues, op. cit., p. 333.

7. *Life*, Ch. 9, 6; Kavanaugh and Rodrigues, op. cit., p. 72.

8. Ibid., Ch. 30, 19, p. 202.

9. *Life,* Ch. 30, 19; Peers, op. cit., p. 203.

10. *Way of Perfection,* Ch. 19, 4; Peers, op. cit., Vol. II. Cf. *Foundations,* Ch. 41; Peers, op. cit., Vol. III, p. 203.

11. Ibid., p. 85.

12. *Relations* 20; Peers, op. cit., Vol. I, p. 344.

13. *Conceptions of the Love of God,* Ch. 7; Peers, op. cit., Vol. II, p. 398.

14. Ibid., pp. 397-398.

15. *Life*, Ch. 9,2; 21,9; 22,19; *Relations* 8,6; 9,9; etc.

16. *Life*, Ch. 14; *Exclamations of the Soul* 7; etc.

17. *Life*, Ch. 25; *Relations* 4; *Interior Castle,* Book 6, Ch. 3.

18. *Life*, Ch. 40.

19. *Way of Perfection,* Ch. 21; Peers, op. cit., Vol. II, p. 90.

20. *Conceptions of the Love of God,* Ch. 1; Peers, op. cit., Vol. II, p. 361.

Chapter Nine: Simone Weil

1. Simone Weil, *Waiting on God* (London: Collins Fontana, 1963), p. 33.

2. See D. Anderson's short biography, *Simone Weil* (London: SCM Press, 1971).

3. S. Weil, op. cit., p. 64.

4. Ibid., p. 61.

5. Ibid., p. 50.

6. Ibid., p. 44.

7. Ibid., p. 45.

8. J. M. Perrin and G. Thibon, "Inspiration Occitanienne," *Simone Weil as We Knew Her* (London: Routledge & Kegan Paul, 1953), p. 64.

9. J. Blenkinsopp, "Frustrated Pilgrim, Afterthoughts on Simone Weil," *Dublin Review* (1961), pp. 277-285;
N. Braybrooke, "Edith Stein and Simone Weil. A Study in Belief," *Spiritual Life* 14 (1968), pp. 241-247;
N. Braybrooke, "Two Spiritual Heroes of the 20th Century," *Catholic Education Today* 6 (1972), pp. 6-8.

10. J. M. Perrin and G. Thibon, *Simone Weil as We Knew Her*, p. 53.

11. Ibid., p. 47.

12. S. Weil, op. cit., p. 19.

13. Ibid., p. 41.

14. Ibid., p. 48.

15. Ibid., pp. 29, 42, 36, 37.

16. Ibid., p. 34.

17. Ibid., p. 35.

18. Ibid., pp. 35-36.

19. Ibid.

20. Ibid., p. 38.

21. Ibid.

22. Ibid., pp. 30-31.

23. E. Ott, "Die 'Aufmerksamkeit' als Grundvollzug der christlichen Meditation," *Geist und Leben* 47 (1974), pp. 94-112;
J. M. Perrin, "Simone Weil et sa doctrine de l'attention," *La Vie Spirituelle* 129 (1975), pp. 835-846.

24. S. Weil, op. cit., p. 72.

25. J. M. Perrin and G. Thibon, *Simone Weil as We Knew Her*, p. 143.

26. S. Weil, op. cit., p. 75.

27. Ibid., p. 66.

28. Ibid., p. 67.

29. J. M. Perrin, *La Vie Spirituelle,* p. 839.

30. J. M. Perrin and G. Thibon, *Simone Weil as We Knew Her,* p. 88.

31. S. Weil, op. cit., p. 74.

32. J. M. Perrin and G. Thibon, *Simone Weil as We Knew Her,* p. 33 [from a private letter].

33. S. Weil, op. cit., pp. 62-63.

34. G. Hourdin, "Simone Weil," *Internationale Katholieke Informatie* 7 (1973), No. 23, pp. 20-22.

35. J. M. Perrin and G. Thibon, *Simone Weil as We Knew Her,* p. 43.

Chapter Ten: Have Time for God

1. *The Bhagavad-Gita,* Ch. 6, 10-14, trans. J. Mascaro (Penguin, 1962), p. 70.

2. *Harijan,* June 1, 1935. Quotations from newspapers in this and ensuing notes are taken from:
   S. R. Tikekar, *Epigrams from Gandhiji* (Delhi: Patiala House, 1971).

3. *Young India,* December 20, 1928.

4. Ibid., September 24, 1931.

5. *Harijan,* December 10, 1938.

6. Ibid., April 28, 1946.

7. Cf. J.N.M. Wijngaards, "Gandhi and Hindu Prayer," *The Outlook* 14 (1974), pp. 103-104, 111.

8. M. Trouncer, *The Gentleman Saint* (London: Catholic Book Club, 1963).

9. *Introduction à la Vie Devote* 2,1 (Paris: Edition Gabalda, 1945), pp. 73-75. The English translation is my own, freely rendered.

10. H. B. Mackey, ed., *Letters to Persons in the World* (London: Burns & Oates, 1880?), p. 61.

11. Ibid., pp. 58, 160, 56.

12. Ibid., p. 79.

13. Ibid., p. 74.

14. Ibid., p. 426.

15. *Introduction à la Vie Devote* 3,24, p. 257.

16. Ibid., 2,8, p. 89.

17. H. B. Mackey, ed., op. cit., p. 352 (translation slightly adapted).

18. Ibid., p. 308.

19. Ibid., pp. 332-333.

20. Ibid., p. 31.

21. Ibid., pp. 312-313.

22. C. Northcote Parkinson, "High Finance," *Parkinson's Law* (Penguin, 1970), p. 60.